$\mathcal{A}$ SOCIETY OF WOLVES
NATIONAL PARKS AND
THE BATTLE OVER THE WOLF

RICK McINTYRE

with forewords by
Senator Ben Nighthorse Campbell and
Jay D. Hair, President, National Wildlife Federation

VOYAGEUR PRESS

Text and photos copyright © 1993 by Rick McIntyre (except where noted).
Lyrics for the song on page 116, "Wolf," copyright © 1988 by Jack Wallace Gladstone (BMI).
Excerpt on page 77 reprinted with permission of Charles Scribner's Sons, an imprint of Macmillan Pub. Co., from *Of Wolves and Men*, copyright © 1978 by Barry Holstun Lopez.
Excerpt on page 96 reprinted with permission of Oxford University Press, from *A Sand County Almanac*, copyright © 1949 by Aldo Leopold.

Edited by Elizabeth Knight and Helene Anderson
Printed in Hong Kong
94 95 96 97 5 4 3

Library of Congress Cataloging-in-Publication Data
McIntyre, Rick.
A society of wolves : national parks and the battle over the wolf / Rick McIntyre.
p. cm.
Includes bibliographical references (p. 123) and index.
ISBN 0-89658-194-2
1. Wolves—North America. 2. National parks and reserves—Government policy—United States. 3. Wildlife management—United States. 4. Wildlife reintroduction—United States. I. Title.
QL737.C22M385 1993
599.75'442—dc20   93-15918
CIP

Published by
VOYAGEUR PRESS, INC.
P.O. Box 338, 123 North Second Street, Stillwater, MN 55082 U.S.A.
Please write or call, or stop by, for our free catalog of natural history publications.
Our toll-free number to place an order or to obtain a free catalog is
800-888-WOLF (800-888-9653), or 612-430-2210 from Minnesota or Canada.

Educators, fundraisers, premium and gift buyers, publicists, and marketing managers:
Looking for creative products and new sales ideas? Voyageur Press books are available at special discounts when purchased in quantities, and special editions can be created to your specifications. For details contact the marketing department.

Facing page: *The limping wolf from the East Fork Pack watching for prey from the rocky slopes of Cathedral Mountain, Denali National Park.*

For the Limping Wolf,
may your line always prosper

If you talk to the animals they will talk with you
and you will know each other.
If you do not talk to them you will not know them,
and what you do not know you will fear.
What one fears one destroys.

CHIEF DAN GEORGE

CONTENTS

Forewords

    By Senator Ben Nighthorse Campbell   6

    By Jay D. Hair, President, National Wildlife Federation   7

Introduction: A Society of Wolves   9

The Wolf through Human Eyes   15

    The Old World • The New World • Europeans in a New World
    Sidebars: The Seasons of the Wolf • The Alpha Pair: Who's the Boss?

The National Parks and the War on the Wolf   47

    Yellowstone and the Idea of the National Park • Glacier National Park
    • The War Against the Wolf
    Sidebar: Duel in Colorado: Bill Caywood versus the Wolf

A Place for Wolves   87

    Changing Attitudes toward Wolves • The Return of Wolves to Glacier National Park
    • Wolves for Yellowstone
    Sidebars: The Wolves of Isle Royale National Park • The Eastern Timber Wolf:
    Maine, New Hampshire, and New York • The Mexican Wolf: On the Brink of
    Extinction • The Red Wolf: A Return to Smoky Mountains National Park
    • Are Wolves Already Back in Yellowstone? • The Wolf Recolonization of
    Washington State • Bringing the Wolf Back to Colorado • Alaska's Proposed
    Aerial Wolf Control Program

Epilogue: The Spirit of a Wolf   115

How to Become Involved with Wolf Issues   119

    Nonprofit Wolf Organizations • Newsletters and Magazines on Wolf Issues
    • Making Your Voice Heard

References and Suggested Reading on Wolves   123

Index   124

Acknowledgments   126

FOREWORDS

RICK MCINTYRE HAS GIVEN US A COMPELLING BOOK on a very important subject, a book that reintroduces modern people to our less domesticated selves and allows us to get reacquainted with our longtime neighbors and family-oriented fellows—the wolves.

With far-ranging, unblinking research and photography, McIntyre's work is reminiscent of the wolf himself. Through these pages we travel to places most of us only dream about going one day, where we can hunt, live, and play among our wolf cousins. A *Society of Wolves* serves up an experience akin to the movie "City Slickers," in which we shed our "civilized" misconceptions and masquerades in order to explore what it means to be alive among other living creatures.

According to the traditions and myths of my own people, the American Indian, the wolf was not to be feared, for he did not (and does not) kill people—or their grandmothers! Rather, the wolf was respected and revered, for his intelligence, his family and even "tribal" orientation, his cleverness, and his coordinating skills in the hunt. Among Indian people and societies, we have many stories, some recounted in this book, that illustrate the bravery of the wolf and tell of the friendly, helpful—and even spiritually illuminating—encounters people have had with Brother Wolf.

This book takes us inside the Indian perspective. Within this world view, which recently is gaining greater understanding and currency among non-Indian North Americans, people seek not so much to dominate the earth and dictate the fate of all who live here with us. Instead, we are compelled to tread less heavily, to seek to live in harmony, respecting the place and importance of each other creature and even the less animate occupants of the planet.

Why shouldn't wolves live in our vast, western national parks, as they did for thousands of years before the advent of fences and a government that "sets aside" natural lands as separate and protected? The answer is, they should. With protection guaranteed for livestock owners, irrational fears of wolves should be subject to the light of day and chased away like so many moonbeams.

I look at the pictures and read the text in this book, and I am in great awe of these magnificent creatures, the wolves, and, indeed, of their society. I see that people can learn valuable lessons from these animals and that wolves deserve the same reverence and good will to which we accord the buffalo and the beaver, the bear and the eagle.

And while people continue to fill up open spaces with suburbs, malls, and golf courses, we should redouble our efforts to preserve our national parks in as undeveloped and natural state as possible so our wild cousins also have somewhere to live.

May there never come a time when a person alone in the wild country could not hear the lonely, yet comforting, cry of the wolf.

COLORADO SENATOR
BEN NIGHTHORSE CAMPBELL
Descendant of the Northern Cheyenne

$\mathcal{N}$OW THAT WE HAVE CONQUERED THIS VAST and wonderful land of ours, we are finally learning to ask how we should come to terms with it.

The story of that conquest is a dramatic sweep of abuse and heroism, of avarice and courage. Within it are found the ballads of American culture: from cavalry and cowboys and Native Americans, to timberjacks, mountain men, and trappers. In modern guise, the odyssey's symbols have been transformed into bulldozer blades and gleaming towers of steel and glass.

Throughout it all, we've never really come to terms with the land. We've been too busy using it up. Now, with so much gone and put to use both good and ill, there is little choice but to seek how we make peace with this place that is our home.

The answer no doubt involves many weighty considerations of law and commerce and custom. But the answer, I believe, resides in our souls. It comes from us and not to us. We are a natural part of the land and all its creations and just as what serves it serves us, what diminishes it diminishes us.

The wolf, by happenstance beyond its own making, has become bound up in all this as a metaphor for both the story of conquest and the search for terms. By its nature, the wolf could not be better cast. Fierce, cunning, resilient, a force that inspires in us both awe and fear, the wolf as predator and social animal uncannily mirrors much that is of our own nature.

Native Americans heeded these similarities by denoting the wolf "brother." Both prospered, until the conquest began. When it did, the wolf became a deliberate target of extermination.

The earliest colonialists brought their aversion to the wolf with them from the Old World. They transplanted a fear of wolves rooted in murky superstitions, tales that mixed werewolves, witches, and sorcery into an evil brew. As the westward expansion grew, other predators like the mountain lion and coyote were stalked as threats to livestock, but none evoked the mysterious frightfulness nor were so thoroughly scourged as the wolf.

From a once thriving population of perhaps two million wolves within the lower forty-eight states, the official and private policy of eradication decimated the wolf to within a breath short of extinction.

Even at Yellowstone, the country's first national park set aside to preserve wildlife and the scenic beauty in which it lives, the wolf had virtually disappeared by the 1920s. The extermination was carried out by any means necessary and was considered work done for the public good. No animal has ever by design been so successfully destroyed within this country as the wolf. By the 1950s, they had become extinct throughout the contiguous states, excepting a few packs that survived in remote forests of the Upper Midwest. The conquest was complete.

If one wished to mark when a change in this bleak attitude began, no better example could be found than the account in these pages of the confrontation between hunter and prey, man and wolf, trapper Bill Caywood and the wolf named Rags the Digger. This single episode, with resonances of William Faulkner's *The Bear*, is a compelling statement of the instinct to endure. It is but one of the stories to which Rick McIntyre brings directness, insight, and something of his own soul in illuminating for us the society of wolves. It is a story richly deserving to be seen and told, and McIntyre does faithful credit to both.

Much of the story that appears here is of a transformation underway as we come to grips with our relationship to the land by reexamining our attitude toward wolves. Just as we have a rightful place in the natural creation, so too do wolves.

Slowly, delicately even, as we come to terms with the land, the wolf is finding its way back into the remaining wilds that are its natural home. This process, resisted by some, would be impossible without the involvement of many individuals who realize that reintroducing wolves to land where they belong requires an affirmative determination by society as a whole.

The National Wildlife Federation is proud of its contributions in concert with other organizations and conservation activists to making the responsible reestablishment of wolves in the wild a reality. This effort both relies upon and is a vindication of a strong Endangered Species Act.

Wolf reintroduction now centers on Yellowstone National Park and portions of its surrounding public lands. This effort is particularly appropriate given Yellowstone's premier rank among those places where wildlife shall flourish permanently in its fully natural state. This saga, as well as successes already achieved for wolf reintroductions and others that are being prepared, are recounted in the pages that follow.

Perhaps from this record some additional insight may be drawn that a first step toward coming to terms with the land is to let go of the impulse to conquer it.

JAY D. HAIR
President, National Wildlife Federation

An adult member of the East Fork wolf pack in Alaska's Denali National Park. The ancestors of the East Fork wolves were intensively studied by Adolph Murie during the late 1930s and early 1940s, when Denali was known as Mount McKinley National Park, in the first large-scale scientific research project ever conducted on wolves.

INTRODUCTION:
A SOCIETY OF WOLVES

STANDING COMPLETELY STILL, THE WOLF STARES STRAIGHT AHEAD. With a slow, fluid motion, it lowers its body into a crouch, then charges forward at a dead run. The wolf races toward the center of a small meadow where an animal lies on the ground, seemingly asleep. On the far side of the meadow, three other pack members burst into view, sprinting toward the same target.

At the same instant, the four wolves strike their prey. Two grab his head while the others attack the flanks. Their victim jumps up and vigorously shakes his body, hurling the wolves from him. Each wolf hits the ground, scrambles to its feet, and flings itself back into the battle. In a moment, all four wolves reattach themselves to their quarry.

Their beleaguered prey, with great effort, again tries to dislodge his attackers. First one wolf, then all four are thrown off. The wolves pause to see what their prey will do. He stares back at his assailants, then slowly limps off a few dozen yards, lies down, and goes to sleep. Losing interest in the game, the wolves trot over to him, curl up, and doze off.

The four wolves are six-week-old pups, and their intended prey was their father, the alpha male of the East Fork Pack in Alaska's Denali National Park. The pups used him to practice their stalking and attacking techniques. The adult willingly played the victim, but walked off when the game grew too painful.

∽

Denali National Park and Preserve, a six-million-acre (9,400-square-mile) wilderness that straddles the Alaska Range, provides sanctuary to hundreds of diverse life forms, ranging from the delicate Arctic poppy to the mighty grizzly bear. Of all the national parks, Denali offers the best chance to glimpse the ultimate symbol of wildness: the gray wolf (*Canis lupus*). The East Fork wolf pack claims an eight-hundred-square-mile section of Denali, centered on the East Fork of the Toklat River, as their territory. For generations, these wolves and their ancestors have trotted across the tundra, earning their living by hunting moose, caribou, and Dall sheep.

Denali, known as Mount McKinley National Park until 1980, was created by Congress in 1917, at the tail end of a great period of park-making by the American people. Our country invented the concept of national parks, an idea that represented a new attitude toward nature. In the midst of settling the West, of civilizing the continent, some far-sighted citizens argued for setting aside and preserving the best examples of wild America. Public opinion supported the proposal, and Congress established a system of national parks, including such crown jewels as Yellowstone, Yosemite, Sequoia, Rocky Mountain, Grand Canyon, Glacier, and McKinley. The natural features and wildlife found within these parks would be protected as a trusted legacy, passed on from one generation to another.

But the early managers of these national parks defined preservation and protection in ways that seem incredible today. The contemporary attitude classified wildlife species as either "good" or "bad" animals. Big game species such as elk, deer, moose, bison, and bighorn sheep fell into the favored category. Park administrators felt that national parks existed to preserve and protect those animals. Anything that threatened them, whether poachers, forest fires, or predators, had to be controlled. Based on that premise, predators, especially wolves, became bad animals, and any action that killed them off could be justified.

Besides wolves, many other animals were also blacklisted and shot, trapped, or poisoned during the early decades of the national park system: mountain lions, lynx, bobcats, red foxes, gray foxes, swift foxes, badgers, wolverines, mink, weasels, fishers, otters, martens, and coyotes. Amazingly, rangers even destroyed pelicans in Yellowstone on the premise of protecting trout.

The predator control program in the national parks was just an extension of a national policy to rid the country of undesirable species. The wolf headed the list of species we vowed to exterminate. From the late 1800s through the first few decades of the twen-

Right: *During the early days of the national parks, park managers felt they had to "protect" game species such as deer, elk, caribou, and pronghorn from wolves and other predators. That attitude led to the extermination of wolves from Glacier and Yellowstone national parks.* Below: *An East Fork wolf scans the tundra for prey such as caribou, moose, Dall sheep, or ground squirrels.*

The East Fork wolves and the other wolf packs in Denali National Park live in one the few North American ecosystems that still contain all the original predator and prey species. For that reason, Denali is an ideal research area for biologists studying predator-prey relationships.

tieth century, individuals, ranching associations, county and state governments, and federal agencies waged unrelenting war on the wolf.

That war against the wolf became one of the most successful government programs ever launched. Before the arrival of European settlers in North America, two million wolves lived in what is now the lower forty-eight states. By the 1930s, wolves had been exterminated in the western states. At their lowest ebb, only a few hundred wolves, living in remote regions of northern Minnesota, remained in the forty-eight contiguous states. From two million to a few hundred: Never has one species so completely waged war on a fellow species.

The East Fork wolves lived through these troubled times and, like other packs, had to cope with humans who sought to destroy them. Martin Cole, in his book, *Journey to Caribouland,* relates an incident that captures the 1930s attitude toward wolves in Mount McKinley National Park. Cole came to Alaska in 1930, looking for work. He landed a job with the Alaska Road Commission, doing survey work on the road that later gave tourists access to McKinley.

Cole and his foreman, a man named Wallace, surveyed a section of the road that passed through the territory of the East Fork Pack. While working that area, the two men saw fifty thousand caribou migrate past them. After describing the herd, Cole added a comment about the local wolves: "Because the wolves were preying heavily on the caribou they were not protected. The park service was anxious to eliminate them. In this respect, Wallace was . . . furnished a Springfield army rifle." The McKinley rangers, in their attempt to "eliminate" the East Fork wolves, loaned a government rifle to the surveyors with instructions to shoot any wolves they saw. The local wolves wisely kept their distance from the crew, and the men never got a chance to shoot one.

Nine years later, in 1939, a federal biologist named Adolph Murie came to McKinley to study wolves. The park service assigned him the job of documenting and analyzing the relationship of wolves to their prey. Future management of wolves, in McKinley and other parks, would be based on Murie's research, the first in-depth scientific study of wolves.

After talking to the local rangers and scouting the terrain, Murie decided to concentrate his studies on the East Fork Pack,

Martin Cole, an employee of the Alaska Road Commission in 1930, watches for a chance to shoot a wolf in Mount McKinley National Park. The rifle had been loaned to him by a park ranger. The policy of killing of wolves in the park continued until 1952. (Photo courtesy of Martin Cole.)

the most visible wolves in the park. In 1944, he published the results of his intensive research in *The Wolves of Mount McKinley*, a book regarded as a milestone in wildlife research. The book details the lives and activities of the East Fork wolves, especially their impact on the local prey species. From his observations of the pack, the biologist discovered that the wolves and their prey lived in a rough balance with each other, a finding that debunked the contemporary belief that predators decimated prey populations.

The Park Service responded to Murie's ground-breaking research by suspending wolf control efforts in McKinley. Antiwolf interests, however, fought this change in policy and demanded that wolves be killed off to save the park's game species. Despite Murie's scientific research on wolf-prey relationships, the Park Service reinstated the wolf control program in 1945 and continued it until 1952. National Park Service historian, William Brown, while researching the history of Mount McKinley/Denali National Park, found records documenting a kill of at least seventy park wolves between 1929 and 1952. Private trappers and government predator control agents killed a significant but unknown number of additional wolves along the park boundary. For that reason, the total

number of park wolves legally taken in control work would be substantially higher than Brown's figure.

Despite efforts to kill them, the East Fork wolves survived and still occupy the same territory their ancestors held fifty-four years ago when Murie began his research. Since Murie's day, other researchers, including Gordon Haber and L. David Mech, the world's leading expert on wolves, have come to Denali to conduct long-term wolf studies on the East Fork wolves and other packs. And it was in Denali during my off-duty hours that I watched the East Fork Pack for fifteen summers, starting in 1976.

During my years in Denali, I often had the privilege of showing fellow park rangers and visitors their first wolf, nearly always an East Fork pack member. Later, virtually every person described the sighting as one of the peak experiences of their lives. Wolves inevitably evoke strong emotional responses in human beings. Some people admire and even idolize the wolf while others hate the animal with a deep intensity. The complex and highly charged relationship between these two societies, wolves and human, is the subject of this book.

The alpha female of the East Fork Pack, mate of the limping male. On this day she took a break from nursing her pups and went on a hunt with the beta male and two other pack members. They killed a caribou but later lost the carcass to an aggressive grizzly bear.

THE WOLF THROUGH HUMAN EYES

*T*HE ALPHA MALE OF THE EAST FORK PACK has an old paw injury that causes a severe limp in his left front leg. When traveling, he usually walks on three legs and holds his wounded foot off the ground. A wolf with that disability would seem a liability to the pack. Would other pack members kill such a cripple? Despite his handicap, the limping male holds his dominant position, and the other wolves defer to him in every circumstance. When the whole pack is out on a hunt, the others periodically wait for the limping male to catch up. They give him their allegiance and never withdraw it.

On this day, the alpha pair is traveling across a broad, flat valley when the female suddenly stops, sniffs the air, and catches sight of a herd of caribou bedded on the tundra. She and her mate immediately sprint toward them. The caribou see the charging wolves, jump up, and easily outrun them. After chasing the herd a few hundred yards, the wolves give up, rest a bit, then continue on their rounds, looking for another opportunity. They find and test several other bands, but are unable to make any kills.

An hour later, they find another caribou herd and charge toward it. At first, it seems that these caribou are also going to escape, but then one young calf falls behind. Recognizing the opportunity, the female wolf shifts to top speed and closes in on the calf. Her mate, hindered by his lame paw, struggles to keep up.

The calf's mother has been running beside her offspring but now sees that the wolves have targeted it. She stays with the calf for a few more moments, then resigning herself to the hopelessness of the situation, distances herself from it.

With every stride, the female wolf gains on the calf. A few seconds later, just as it is about to be seized, the calf collapses, and the alpha female immediately kills it. The limping male joins his mate, and they feast on the carcass. This has been an easy kill, but it comes only after many failed attempts. The wolves have run far and worked hard for their meal.

∾

Above: An East Fork wolf watching a small herd of caribou. The wolf never chased the group. Perhaps it sensed that all these caribou were healthy, prime animals, easily capable of outrunning a wolf. Right: A male wolf howling to a female wolf out of his sight. Early humans may have developed cooperative hunting strategies and long-distance communication techniques based on their observations of wolf packs.

Above: An East Fork mother wolf carrying a piece of caribou meat to her litter.

THE OLD WORLD

There is no sound quite like the howl of a wolf or the wild harmonies created by a pack of wolves. While out on the tundra, I often heard the East Fork wolves calling out to each other. For me, it was a great privilege to eavesdrop on their conversations and guess at their meanings. Once, as I listened to them, I thought about how my Scottish ancestors might have reacted to the sound of a wolf howl, as it reverberated across the mountains and moors of their Highland home. For them, a howl would have been a threatening sound—one that likely induced an involuntary shudder.

My clan settled a remote Scottish valley named Glen Coe in the tenth century. Like most other Highlanders, they became crofters, the local name for tenant farmers. Each family worked a handful of acres that supported a few crops and a meager collection of livestock, perhaps one cow and several sheep. No one could afford to lose an animal. If a wolf killed the stock, the family could starve. The only way to protect the animals was to bring them into the family's tiny cottage for the night.

The howl of a wolf not only foreshadowed the possible loss of livestock, it also was interpreted as an imminent threat to any person still out in the fields or moors. Highlanders feared that wolves would hunt down and kill a clan member foolish enough to be out in the night.

Human society in Europe did not always feel threatened by wolves. Ice Age hunters often came into contact with wolf packs. Both species pursued the same big game in the same areas. Based on what we know of more recent hunter-gatherer cultures, the relationship between early European humans and wolves was likely a respectful and fairly peaceful competition. Since habitat and game were abundant, both types of social predators could afford to be tolerant of each other. As wolf biologist Ed Bangs put it, early humans and wolves were "brothers in the hunt."

People and wolves lived in societies that were very similar. Both species shared such characteristics as pair-bonding, extended family clans, group cooperation to achieve goals, communal care and training of young (by both males and females), group ceremonies, leadership hierarchies, and perhaps most notably, the sense of kinship that caused individuals to share food with others. In addition, wolf packs, like human clans, sometimes had to defend their territory from others of their kind. Some behaviorists and biologists conclude that, in social customs and subsistence lifestyle, wolves were the prime role models for early humans. In fact, in 1925, Carveth Read of the University of London published a book entitled *Origins of Man*. Read suggested that early humans be given the scientific name *Lycopithecus*, Greek for "wolf-ape." The name implies that our distant ancestors were originally apes who left the

forest and learned to function like a wolf pack in hunting methods and social organization. "Man," wrote Read, "is more like a wolf . . . than he is like any other animal." Perhaps we should think of ourselves as naked wolves rather than naked apes.

The coexistence of the two species lasted until the time people switched to an economy based on farming and tending of livestock. Having a dependable food supply enabled the human race to multiply at an exponential rate, and that population increase radically changed the face of the world. The steppes, meadows, and forests that once provided habitat for game gradually were converted into cropland and pasture. With far less land and food to support the original levels of wild game, their populations crashed.

Although people no longer had to rely on wild animals for sustenance, wolves still had to hunt to live. The dwindling of their prey populations forced many wolves to switch to different targets. They discovered that it was easy to kill the inattentive and slow-moving domestic animals clustered around the human settlements. It took little effort to bring down an animal large enough to feed a whole pack.

The wolves hunted whatever was available. To them, anything on four legs was fair game, but to farmers, the theft of their livestock was an unforgivable crime. The two species, formerly brothers in the hunt, now were direct rivals.

Continued loss of range and wild game forced greater numbers of wolves to draw close to farms and villages. Wolves and people encountered each other more frequently than ever before. Horrifying rumors of wolves killing humans spread among settlements.

Stories of wolf attacks on people in Europe and Russia are difficult to verify due to lack of documentation. Nearly all the accounts seem greatly exaggerated. Whatever the reality, residents of Eurasia certainly believed that wolves regularly killed people. The problem confronting a historian or researcher is that no proven records exist of healthy wild wolves killing people in North America, despite numerous opportunities to do so. Were medieval reports of wolves preying on humans false? Or, was there something happening with Old World wolves that never occurred with North American wolves?

It is now generally believed that wolf-dog hybrids caused many of the human fatalities. The proximity of wolves and dogs, both domestic and feral, in Europe presented many opportunities for hybridization to occur. The offspring of a wolf and a dog are far more dangerous to people than wild wolves because such hybrids lack the wariness of humans most wolves show. During recent times, such crossbreeds, even when kept as house pets, have attacked a number of people. In medieval Europe, at a time when wolves were hated, people immediately blamed them for every attack com-

(continued on page 24)

Right: Many ancient warrior cultures, such as the Roman Empire, revered the wolf. The left-hand section of this 900 A.D. ivory carving kept in the Vatican shows a wolf nursing Romulus and Remus, twin children of the god Mars. Romulus later founded the city of Rome, and the image of a nursing wolf become a symbol of their empire. Above the wolf is a depiction of Christ on the cross. What better way to illustrate the victory of Christianity over paganism than to show the cross hovering triumphantly over a wolf? In addition, because Christ was the ultimate symbol of good, this piece of art implies that the wolf is the ultimate symbol of evil, a concept widely believed in medieval Europe. (Photo courtesy of Scala/Art Resource, NY.)
Above: The intense yellow eyes of the wolf caused many humans to believe that wolves had strange supernatural powers.

The Seasons of the Wolf

SPRING

The life of a wolf begins underground, in the seclusion of a den. The mother wolf is usually her pack's alpha female, the top-ranking female. A typical litter contains six pups, each weighing about one pound.

For the first two weeks the sightless, deaf pups live in a small, dark, but cozy world. They stay in constant contact with each other and their mother who warms them by curling herself around their tiny bodies. When hungry, each pup wiggles about until it finds a nipple, then nurses.

Lack of sight and hearing intensifies the pups' senses of touch. They will always remember the warmth, security, and good feelings they got from direct contact with their siblings and mother. Years later, as adults, they will seek out the closeness and touch of other pack members.

On occasion, the pups sense their mother's mood change to a state of great excitement. Pups positioned near her rear end find themselves struck repeatedly by her wagging tail. She is reacting to a visitor, her mate, the alpha male, coming to bring her food. After an affectionate greeting, he pauses for a quick sniff of the pups, then backs out of the den. The mother wolf is completely dependent on her mate and other pack members for support during her confinement in the den.

By the third week, the pups' eyes have opened, and in the dim light of the den, they begin to make out the shapes of their mother and littermates. Then, one by one, the pups climb up to the den's entrance and tumble out into a new and unfamiliar world. As they timidly emerge, the pups immediately attract the attention of nearby adult wolves.

Pack members rush over to greet and sniff each pup. For the first time, the pups experience what it means to be part of a pack. Through this early socializing, each pup forms strong emotional attachments to its littermates and to adult pack members.

In all the excitement, the pups do not notice the disappearance of their mother. Finally freed from the den, she romps with abandon in the sun. She then shares a quick hunt with her mate, a brief adventure that renews their bond.

During the parents' absence, every surrounding adult competes for a chance to care for the pups. In some wolf packs, nonbreeding females produce milk and nurse the pups when the mother is away. One or two adults, in an effort to please the pups, regurgitate their last meal and offer it to the litter. The pups sniff the meat but are not yet ready to eat the semisolid material.

For the next few weeks, the pups divide their time between the den and the surface world. Soon they begin sleeping outside and exploring the surrounding countryside, usually by tagging along after an indulging adult.

When not eating or sleeping, the pups play with each other. Sometimes just two at a time, sometimes all together, the pups invent and engage in endless varieties of games. They chase each other, fight, and stage tug-of-war contests. Play is the perfect way to develop their strength, agility, and coordination. Equally important, the playful fights and competitive games begin the process that eventually establishes each pup's place in the pack's hierarchy.

As the pups play around the den, they pick up and carry around bits of meat, hide, and bone. Each pup soon senses that some of these items are edible and swallows the tastier pieces. The scraps also become pretend prey, and the pups practice their stalking and hunting skills by attacking them.

In addition to their games and mock hunting sessions, the pups romp with older members of the pack. The adults show great tolerance when the pups roughhouse with them. Any pup that becomes too aggressive is just shaken off or momentarily pinned to the ground. In such ways, the older wolves use their superior size and strength to show that they can physically dominate the pups if they choose.

During this period of intense activity, the mother's milk supply does not fully satisfy the pups' appetites. The pups tentatively sample the regurgitated food the adults offer them. Once they taste it, they immediately want more. The pups instinctively rush up to any incoming adult, excitedly lick its mouth, whine, and wag their tails. The adult responds by disgorging its last meal. After quickly bolting down the meat, the pups run over to the next adult and demand another helping.

Within two months of birth, the pups are weaned and eating a variety of solid food. They now are about one-third adult size and ready for the next stage of their integration into wolf society, a stage that will take them away from their den and further out into the world.

Top left: *A three-week-old wolf pup relaxing near the entrance to its den. At this age, pups begin interacting with other pack members, a process that teaches them their place in the society of wolves.* Top right: *A four-week-old pup timidly explores a shallow stream near its den.* Bottom: *The mother wolf and one of the four-week-old pups outside their den. The pup later got lost when it wandered away from the den and the mother had to carry it back home in her mouth.*

Note: *All close-up photos of wolf pups in this book were taken of animals born in captivity. No wild wolf den should ever be approached, as the adult pack members will likely attempt to move their pups to a safer location. Some of the pups may not survive such a stressful move.*

SUMMER

When the pups are eight to ten weeks old, the adult wolves round them up and herd them a few miles cross-country to a prechosen location. As soon as the trip is over, the pups, exhausted from their first long-distance foray, plop down and go to sleep. For the next few months, this spot will be the pack's summer home and rendezvous site, sort of an open-air nursery. If the parents both go on a hunt, a babysitter, often a yearling, stays behind to tend the pups. When a pack member makes a kill, it brings back a portion to the rendezvous site to share with the pups. Besides feeding the pups, adult wolves frequently give food to the yearlings who helped care for the litter.

Wolf researchers John Fentress and Jenny Ryon have documented an extraordinary aspect of social bonding within a pack called "relay feeding." During a study of a captive pack, the biologists observed yearlings taking the food they had received from the adults and sharing it with the pups. What makes this sharing behavior even more amazing is the fact that the yearlings were not related to the alpha pair or the pups. The previous year, as three-month-old pups, they had been adopted by the alphas. This sharing and relaying of food from adult wolves to yearlings to pups perfectly illustrates the depth of social bonding and communal care within a wolf pack.

As the pups mature, they become more aware of the social interactions within the pack. They watch as the adults greet and socialize with each other and notice which wolves are dominant over others. They take in the subtle facial and body language that reveals the dominant or submissive position of a wolf. When a low-ranking wolf fails to defer properly to a higher-ranking animal, the pups witness the swift but brief punishment. Gradually, they learn the rules that establish order and keep the peace in wolf society.

The pups also discover the separate dominance hierarchies that rule the male and female members of the pack. The alpha male, the pups' father, is the dominant male in the pack. His mate, the alpha female, is the top female. When either alpha animal chooses to, it can exert its will over others in the pack, either by force of personality or physical force.

Although the alphas use aggression to maintain their rank, prolonged and injurious fighting among pack members is rare. When I watched the East Fork wolves interacting in Alaska, I saw that friendliness, not aggression, was the predominant behavior among pack members.

Within the litter, the pups have already begun to work out their miniaturized version of the social structure of the pack. One pup has probably taken on the role of the alpha animal and tries to dominate all the fights and wrestling matches. The hierarchy in the litter, however, often reshuffles. The lines of dominance will not be clearly sorted out until the pups reach breeding age, several years later.

Far top: *A six-week-old pup.* Far bottom: *Nine-week-old pups playing. This litter has already worked out a social hierarchy among its four members.* Below: *The mother wolf and her fourteen-week-old pup with a freshly killed jackrabbit.* Left: *Fourteen-week-old pups resting after playing.*

The alpha wolves usually are the parents of most of the other pack members. The parental care and training given by the alphas strongly imprints their position of dominance in the minds of each generation of pups. On growing up, they will find it difficult to challenge their parents' authority. Their relationship to the alphas is much like that of a dog puppy to its owner. The puppy treats its owner as if he or she is an alpha wolf. Even when grown to adult size and strength, the dog still regards its owner as dominant.

Training in hunting techniques begins in late summer when the pups follow an adult out on a short hunting trip. As the party travels along, the older wolf stops frequently to examine scents. Imitating the adult, the pups sniff the same scents and try to decipher their meanings. On spotting a prey animal, the adult gives chase. The pups enthusiastically join the pursuit, but their limited stamina causes them to lag behind. If the adult catches the prey, it most likely will share the food with its apprentices. In such ways, the pups learn the fundamentals of hunting from an expert at the game.

As fall approaches, the adults abandon the rendezvous site and take the pups, now old enough to keep up, on long hunts. For the next seven to eight months, the pack will live a nomadic life, roaming at will throughout its territory. Up to this point, the pups have had an easy life. All the other pack members have fed and attended them. Now the adults force the pups to become productive, contributing members of the pack.

mitted by any animal vaguely wolflike in appearance.

Like people, canines suffer from infectious diseases, one of which is rabies. Foxes, dogs, wolves, and other animals that contract rabies may attack people. During the Middle Ages, wolves and wolf-dog hybrids regularly came into contact with rabid dogs and other infected animals. Such contact facilitated the spread of the rabies virus from host to host. Most wolf biologists and historians think that rabies was the primary cause for wolf attacks on humans in the Old World.

The case, however, is quite different in the New World because North American wolves rarely contract rabies. In a recent year, 9,943 confirmed cases of rabies occurred in the United States, Mexico, and Canada. Only three of those animals were wolves. Minnesota, a state with as many as 1,750 wolves, has never had a documented case of rabies in a wild wolf. Mark Johnson, a veterinarian working at Yellowstone National Park in Wyoming, has written that the average rate of human rabies cases in the United States and Canada is less than one person per year.

As frightened as medieval people were of wolves, something far more terrifying lurked through woods, moors, and minds. A howl in the night might be the call of a werewolf, an Old English word that meant "man-wolf." The thought of a man or woman turning into a wolf and brutally killing anyone who crossed its path was one of the greatest abominations a medieval person could contemplate. The demonic transformations had to happen; plenty of "evidence" proved the existence of werewolves.

That evidence, almost never firsthand, rarely was critically examined. There were stories of people acting in blasphemous ways, ways that were bestial and wolflike. Gossip spread of men who bragged that they had the power to become wolves and used that power to murder at will. People said they heard eyewitnesses describe wolf-to-man or man-to-wolf transformations. Secular and religious authorities frequently announced the public torture and execution of known werewolves. Many of the accused confessed to their crime. What more proof of werewolfism was needed? Looking back, can we see that such uncritical acceptance of werewolf stories by medieval people casts further doubt on their belief in rumors of wolves killing large numbers of people?

The abnormal wolfish behavior could be ascribed to a mental illness known as lycanthropy. Its victims believe that they are wild beasts, run on all fours, eat raw meat, howl continually, and act violently. Mass hysteria, the same type that dominated the Salem witch trials, likely gave rise to the supposed eyewitness accounts and voluntary confessions. Confessions extracted under torture only proved that people subjected to extreme pain would admit to anything.

Werewolf hysteria gripped Europe for much of the 1500s and 1600s. People had hated wolves before, but now there was a crusade against anything wolflike. It was not just a fight for security, it was a holy war pursued by human society, the forces of good, against wolves and werewolves, the forces of evil.

As in most cases of hatred and intolerance, what people most despised in wolves and their wolf-man counterparts was something that lay within every human. All of us are capable of yielding to our personal dark side. Werewolves supposedly gave free reign to that bestial nature. They freely acted out what nearly every person sometimes wished he or she could do. The war on wolves was really a war on what people most feared about their own natures. The wolf was a scapegoat. By destroying wolves, a person symbolically destroyed part of his or her sinful nature and came that much closer to redemption.

Virtually every European nation declared war on wolves. The British Isles serves as a good example of how that war progressed. In the second century B.C., the Scottish king Dorvadilla offered an ox to anyone who killed a wolf. A tenth-century English king demanded that the King of Wales pay him a yearly tribute of three hundred wolf pelts. Henry III, in the thirteenth century, gave land grants to vassals who pledged to destroy all wolves in their region. During some periods of British history, taxes and fines could be paid in wolf heads or tongues.

In seventeenth-century Ireland (the country was then known as "Wolfland," a nickname referring to its high wolf population), a bounty of six pounds, an enormous sum at the time, was offered for wolves. Wolf hunts became a favored sport of the ruling class, and nobles bred Irish wolfhounds to run down and kill wolves.

These methods of persecution failed to eliminate the wolf from the British Isles. Scottish historian A. W. Harding wrote of the final solution to the wolf problem: "If the wolf could not be exterminated by normal hunting methods then their lairs, the forests, must be put to the flame. Thus by the end of the sixteenth century the great forests of Rannoch and Lochaber were slowly reduced to ash." Highlanders hated wolves so much they burnt down forest after forest, denying the wolves any sanctuary.

My ancestors participated in this war on wolves. Members of my clan served the English landowning nobility as foresters and gamekeepers. Those positions involved a duty to hunt down and kill any predator that threatened game and livestock. They also would have helped to burn down nearby forests.

The English and Scottish traits of organization and thoroughness eventually prevailed over the perceived enemy. The last wolf in England perished in the early 1500s, and the final Highland wolf died in 1743, not far from my ancestors' glen. No doubt, news of its demise caused much celebration.

Lon Chaney Jr. played the title character in the 1940 Universal Studios film The Wolfman, *a modern retelling of the medieval legend of the werewolf. (Photo copyright © by Universal Studios, Inc. Courtesy of MCA Publishing Rights, a division of MCA, Inc.)*

The native people of North America had an attitude toward wolves that was vastly different from the view held by European people. Wolves lived in nearly all parts of the continent, so almost every tribe had direct contact with them. Indians saw wolves as thinking, reasoning fellow beings that possessed souls. They called the wolf "brother" and treated it with great respect and honor. Their relationship with wolves was likely very similar to the way Ice Age inhabitants of Europe perceived the wolf.

The similarities between wolves and humans were especially obvious to Indians. Like them, the wolf was a hunter, and it lived in a pack that was much like a tribe. The pack functioned as a hunting party and, when necessary, as a war party. The alpha wolf acted like a chief.

Every tribe believed that the wolf had great supernatural power. Hunters and warriors prayed to be granted the stamina of the wolf. The Blackfeet Indians wore wolf skins and sang songs to wolves, hoping that some of the wolf's power would be shared with them. To them, the wolf was a "medicine animal," the highest honor they could ascribe to a fellow creature.

In 1991 and 1992, I lived on the edge of the Blackfeet Indian Reservation in Montana. While studying the tribe's history and culture, I found many references to wolves, especially in books written by James Willard Schultz, a hunter and trapper who lived with the Blackfeet in the late 1800s. In a collection of his writings called *Why Gone Those Times?*, Schultz transcribes the words of Red Eagle as he explained why his people admired wolves:

> Wolves are not like dogs, you know. A dog father knows not his own children. A wolf marries and he and his wife live always together until death. When children come he hunts for them, and brings food for them, and watches over them faithfully while the mother goes out to hunt and run around and keep up her strength. Ah, they are wise, true hearted animals, the big wolves of the plains. And what hunters they are; they never suffer from want of food.

An elder of the Blackfeet, Takes-Gun-Ahead, told Schultz a story called "Old Man and the Wolves." Old Man saw a band of six wolves and called out to them, "My younger brothers! I am very lonely! Take pity on me: let me be a wolf with you!" The father wolf granted Old Man his request and turned him into a wolf. After the transformation, the wolf introduced his family with these words:

And now let me tell you something about our family. My wife and I don't hunt much. Your two younger brothers there are the runners and killers, and their sisters help in the way of heading off and confusing the game. Your younger brother there, Long Body, is the swiftest runner, but he hasn't the best of wind. However, he generally overtakes and kills whatever he chases. Your other younger brother, Heavy Body, is not a fast runner, but he has great staying power, never gets winded, and in the end brings down his prey.

This story, and others like it, portrays the adventures of an Indian who becomes a wolf-man. Nearly always, the main character gains great knowledge and spiritual enlightenment from his experiences. In European legends, a person who turns into a wolf-man inevitably becomes a bloodthirsty killer and a threat to human society. Such diametrically opposed mythology says much about how the two cultures viewed wolves.

In his book, *Blackfeet and Buffalo*, Schultz told how he and a warrior named Eagle Head once witnessed a wolf pack attack a bison. The two men came on the scene just as a big gray wolf spotted an old bison bull. After staring at the bull, the wolf howled four times and was answered by other wolves. Eagle Head turned to his companion and said, "He is calling his relatives."

Soon six wolves joined the first one. The pack, before doing anything else, joyously greeted and played with each other. On finishing their affectionate ceremony, they trotted down to the huge bull and surrounded him. Eagle Head gave a running commentary on the action, explaining to his partner that the first wolf was the leader of the pack. As the pack watched the bull, Eagle Head said that the wolf leader was planning the strategy of the attack.

Then, following the leader's cue, the pack leaped at the bison—two attacked his head as the others bit into his flanks. Although the old bull fought hard—spinning around and lunging at the nearest wolf—he had no real hope; the pack coordinated its attack too well. Whenever the bull tried to gore one wolf, other pack members attacked from the rear. The bull, bleeding from many wounds, soon gave up the fight and the pack quickly dispatched him.

Such accounts stressing the strong family ties of a wolf pack and the way the pack cooperates during the hunt reveal the great respect Indians have for wolves. But perhaps more than any other trait, Native Americans admired the wolf for its ability to endure. Every tribe, wherever it lived, experienced a constant struggle to survive. Indians, through generations of harsh firsthand experience, knew how tough it was to live off the land. When they looked

Adult wolves, brother and sister, at play. The playfulness of this fellow species especially impressed members of the Blackfeet Tribe, the great bison hunters of the northern plains.

at the wolf, they saw a brother who prevailed due to its stamina, intelligence, loyalty to its pack, fierce defense of its territory, and indomitable will to live. Those traits, whether found in a person or wolf, deserved the highest level of respect.

The Indian view of wolves included a sophisticated understanding of ecology and balance of nature. When Eagle Head watched the wolves attack the bison, his companion, James Schultz, grew angry. Feeling that the wolves were unfairly ganging up on the bull, he raised his rifle, aimed at the wolves and told Eagle Head, "It is not fair. I am going to save him!" Quickly grabbing the rifle, Eagle Head told the white man:

> It is his time to die. It is not for us to interfere. Old Man, the World Maker, created buffalo for food for men and wolves. Should you save this old and worn-out bull from them, they would only travel on and pull down the next one—and it, perhaps, a young cow that we may need one day.

Wolves in the New World pose no threat to humans. Schultz and his Blackfeet companions knew this from personal experience.

In *Blackfeet and Buffalo*, Schultz described the contemporary attitude on wolves and their possible threat to people:

> So far as I can learn, the wolves of North America never attacked human beings. There was good reason for it: game animals and birds were everywhere so plentiful that they had no need to attack their greater enemy man. The Indians have no tales about big, bad wolves. They frighten their children into good behavior by threatening them with the bear. Until the late 1870s wolves fairly swarmed upon the Montana plains; their long-drawn melancholy howls were ever in our ears. But lone hunters, both Indians and white, when caught out at night and far from home, lay down to sleep without the slightest fear of them.

When Indians told stories, wolves often appeared as heroic characters willing to help people in trouble. The story of "Sits-By-The-Door and The Medicine Wolf," as told by Brings-Down-The-Sun and reported in Walter McClintock's *The Old North Trail*, is typical. The Crows capture Sits-By-The-Door, a young mother liv-

(continued on page 36)

FALL

During their travels with the pack, the pups receive intensive lessons on communications (especially using scent), and on the meaning of territory. They discover that their pack lives within a well-defined area and that rival wolf packs have territories in adjacent areas. This is a critical point to understand; if a wolf trespasses into another pack's range, it may be killed.

As the pups run with the pack they notice that the adults, particularly the alpha pair, frequently pause to scent mark conspicuous objects. The strong scent of urine, feces, or body rubbing remains for weeks and conveys an obvious message to any foreign wolf: "This area is claimed by a pack and will be defended."

Scent marking also functions as a communication system within the pack. On sniffing a scent, a wolf receives the equivalent of a memo from the fellow pack member who left the mark. The message would be dated (based on the strength of the scent) and convey information on the author's identity and activities. Researcher Roger Peters believes that a network of scent stations within a territory can act as an orientation system, enabling a wolf to know where it is at any given time.

The pups also learn how to communicate through howling. A group howl tells nearby packs or lone wolves that the territory is occupied. If two adjacent packs happen to both be traveling near a common boundary, howling enables each group to lay claim to its respective territories and discourage trespassing.

Eventually, the adults and pups will come across another pack near their boundary. If one group has just made a kill or is more aggressive than the other, a violent confrontation may erupt. Border disputes can cause the death of wolves.

The territorial system is a social mechanism that regulates wolf populations. The number of good territories is limited, and only so many wolves can be sustained in each territory. Under natural conditions, the availability of space and food (both abundance of prey species and the supply of vulnerable individuals) controls the wolf population.

A wolf needs to belong to a pack for hunting efficiency as well as for self-defense. A lone wolf might get by on small-sized prey, but it takes group cooperation to consistently bring down large animals. As the pack trots across its territory, each adult wolf is primed to detect prey. The pack members attune themselves to any scent, sight, sound, or track that might tip them off to a potential target.

Based on wolf research records from throughout the North American continent, a pack that manages to kill 5 to 10 percent of the prey it targets is doing well. For a wolf pack, the most practical hunting strategy is to test a large number of prey for vulnerable individuals. When chasing caribou, the East Fork wolves quickly give up once they see the herd members fleeing at normal speed. Only when one animal lags behind do the wolves continue the pursuit, concentrate on the vulnerable individual, and kill it.

Wolves, like all predators, kill the easiest prey available to them. Studies on wolves regularly show that they concentrate their kills among the youngest, oldest, and sickest of their prey species. An adult animal in prime condition can normally either outrun or, in the case of a moose or a bison, fight off a pack. When wolves kill an animal in its prime years, the prey usually is less fit than others. An injury, an infection, a disease, a parasitic infestation, or an arthritic condition would make an animal less able to escape or fight off a wolf pack.

Although wolves seek out vulnerable prey, that doesn't mean that they never kill healthy animals in their prime. Unusual conditions can put an animal at a disadvantage and give wolves an edge. For example, a strong animal may flounder in a deep snowdrift and be unable to outrun a pack. But, it is far easier for wolves to find and kill something that has a weakness. Ultimately, it is a game of percentages. Wolves continually test prey, gladly accept whatever luck comes their way, and manage to win often enough to ensure the survival of their species.

Because wolves cull inferior members of a prey population, the survivors, the fitter individuals, end up with more space and food. When they breed, their young will also have more forage and room. By pruning out the weaker, least fit individuals, the wolves unknowingly help the fittest individuals and their descendants to prosper. This process of strengthening the genetic viability of a prey species is the antithesis of the type of big-game hunting that kills off the trophy size male members of a wildlife species, the biggest and fittest males, the ones who should be contributing their superior genes to the breeding pool.

All these hunting experiences and strategies are acted out in front of the pups. By now, they have the endurance to participate in the chases but still have to learn how the pack functions as a unit to make kills. One wolf may be especially good at sensing prey. Another, probably an alpha male or female, may be adept at figuring out how to ambush the quarry. A third pack member may possess the speed to catch up with the fleeing animal and make first contact. Finally, the strongest wolf, one that may not have the swiftness to outrun the prey, may be the one that dispatchs the victim as other pack members restrain it. However the wolves coordinate the kill, it will be a group effort in which each wolf plays an important role.

Right top: An alpha male urinating on a tree. Wolf researchers call this behavior "raised leg urination," a sign of dominant status. Right bottom: A group of twenty-week-old pups sharing dinner at a deer carcass. By this age, pups will begin to join older pack members on hunting trips.

WINTER

Nothing would seem harder than to be a wolf trudging through deep snow in the dead of winter, looking for something to hunt and eat. In many areas occupied by wolves, winter temperatures can drop to -70 degrees Fahrenheit. Regardless of the severity of the climate, a wolf has to endure the weather and earn a living.

Luckily for the wolves, the deeper the snow gets, the more vulnerable the prey becomes. After a heavy snowfall, game find it exhaustingly difficult to reach good forage. Deep snow levels combine with poor nutrition to gradually weaken prey. A weakened moose, elk, deer, or caribou gives a pack a much greater chance of making a kill. Wolf studies show that packs consistently kill a higher percentage of targets during severe winters. Thus, for most wolf packs, extreme winter weather guarantees more successful hunting.

By now, the nine-month-old pups are nearly adult-size in body height, but still need another year to fill out their frames. They have learned the basics of wolf society and should be functioning as contributing members of their pack. There is one aspect of their society the pups have yet to experience: the mating season.

For most packs, the breeding season starts in February. The first sign of the season is a dramatic renewal of pair-bonding by the alpha wolves. Both animals forsake many of their normal activities to affectionately devote themselves to their relationship. The pair travels together, plays frequently, grooms each other, and sleeps side by side. Joint scent marking, a sure sign of pair-bonding, becomes a frequent ceremony.

Both alpha wolves then become more aggressive toward other adults in the pack. The alpha female attacks any female that shows an interest in her mate. Males that approach the alpha female are challenged by her mate. The alpha female continually monitors the breeding condition of the other females. If they come into heat, she forcibly prevents them from mating. Normally the alpha female succeeds, and she will be the only female to produce pups.

Although the custom among wolves is for just the alpha pair to reproduce, biologists have reported that alpha males sometimes relinquish their right to breed to another pack member. This is an astonishing behavior, very rare in wild animals. Why would a dominant male give up his breeding privileges, a right that other species violently fight over?

Some researchers theorize that if the alpha female prefers to mate with a different male, the alpha male steps aside. Whatever the reasons behind his "good sportsmanship" behavior, the alpha male appears to care and provide for the other male's pups as well as he would for his own. Similar exceptions have been seen with alpha females who forego breeding for unknown reasons. In such cases, the alpha female helps to care for the pups born to a subordinate female, pups the alpha male likely fathered.

The territorial organization of wolves controls population growth by limiting the number of packs. Since no territory can provide a pack with unlimited food, the alphas must regulate the number of wolves in their territory. If the wolves are near the carrying capacity of their range, limiting breeding to one female will likely produce about the right number of pups to replace adult pack members who have died or dispersed (left the group). In other circumstances, if the prey base can support more wolves, the alpha female might allow a second female, probably one of her daughters, to breed and raise a litter of pups.

Because a wolf pack is usually composed of closely related animals, the group effort to raise the pups is really a family effort. The nonbreeding adults who hunt and babysit for the pups are likely the pups' older brothers and sisters. Their efforts enhance the survival of their common genetic line. The experience of helping to care for the pups is ideal training for raising their own litters if they later become breeders.

The stress and tension created during the mating season can cause some older wolves to leave the pack. A mature male or female may have such a strong desire to breed that he or she will take off and try to find a mate. Yearlings and two-year-olds also may decide to leave the pack and strike out on their own.

A dispersing wolf, on finding a vacant range, will then try to attract a mate. The wolf's solitary scent mark conveys its "single" status to any passing lone wolf. If two wolves pair up, they use double scent marks to claim the vacant area as their territory. In other cases, two dispersing wolves find each other first, then jointly search for a suitable unoccupied territory.

A wolf that leaves the security of its pack is taking a big risk. In country where established packs fully occupy the land, a dispersing wolf has to cross through the territories of many rival packs before it can find a vacant area. That passage would be as dangerous as a lone inner-city gang member walking through the turf of enemy gangs. Occasionally, neighboring packs accept dispersing wolves. If a female meets up with a pack that is top-heavy with males, she may immediately become an alpha female. An experienced male, on contacting a small pack, may be recruited and allotted a high-ranking position.

Researchers have tracked many radio-collared wolves after they left their packs. Some traveled hundreds of miles in search of a vacant range. One wolf, collared by biologist Steve Fritts in Minnesota, later turned up in Saskatchewan, Canada, a straight-line distance of 550 miles. Several Denali radio-collared wolves who failed to find territories returned to their original packs. Their families accepted these prodigals when they reappeared.

In any typical litter of pups, some will always stay with their pack. A pup that becomes dominant over its littermates has a good chance of eventually inheriting an alpha position. Biologists call

Above: *Three wolves at the start of breeding season. The female on the right has just come into heat. She and the female to her left later fought with each other over breeding rights.* Right: *The female wolf in heat, trying to get a male interested in her. The male later rejected her for the female shown in the center of the photo above.*

Left: *A fourteen-year-old female wolf.* Right: *Two wolf pups, twenty weeks old, ignoring a threat display by their pack's alpha male. The pups are hoping the male will feed them.* Above: *A dominance fight between two female wolves. The black female eventually established dominance over all the other females in the pack and became the alpha female. The following spring she produced her first litter of pups.*

these wolves "biders" because they stay home, biding their time, deferring reproduction in hopes that they will become breeders when their parents die.

The path to alpha status may include an apprenticeship at the beta level. In this position, a wolf outranks all other pack members except the alpha pair. Large packs often separate into subunits to hunt. When this happens, the beta male or female may get to lead one of the groups. Alpha males sometimes appear to give beta males a chance to develop their leadership skills. During some hunts, the alpha seems to hold back when prey appears. The beta male then leads the attack and, if possible, makes the kill. Such an experience not only trains the beta male but also gets the pack accus-

tomed to accepting him in a leadership position. The alpha female, as she oversees reproduction and pup raising, may give another female, perhaps a daughter, special preference when it comes to sharing rearing duties.

By the time the next litter is born, the pups from the previous year will be fully integrated into wolf society. They will work with the adults to care for the new pups, their younger brothers and sisters. Some yearlings may specialize in babysitting while others devote extra time to hunting so they can help feed the pups. Each wolf has a role in pack functions, a role that may differ from wolf to wolf, but one that significantly contributes to the welfare of the pack, the society of wolves.

Above: *The mother wolf watching over her pups.* Left: *A wolf family with twenty-week-old pups. The father wolf is on the right, and the mother on the left. Native elders such as Takes-Gun-Along told stories of wolf families that stressed their similarities to human families.*

Above left: *Alpha male wolf. Native North Americans honored the wolf, a species they called brother. As Senator Ben Nighthorse Campbell wrote of his Northern Cheyenne ancestors, ". . . the wolf was respected and revered, for his intelligence, his family and even 'tribal' orientation, his cleverness, and his coordinating skills in the hunt." Above right: Alpha female wolf. Right: Wolf jumping over bush. Prior to the arrive of European colonists, two million wolves lived in what is now the lower forty-eight states.*

ing in a Blackfeet village, and take her two hundred miles away to their camp. She manages to escape but lacks food for her long journey home. When she thinks all hope is lost, a big wolf approaches and lies at her feet.

The woman speaks to the wolf, "Pity me, brother wolf! I am so weak for food that I must soon die. I pray for the sake of my young children that you will help me." Seeming to ignore her request, the wolf trots away and disappears from her sight. Soon he returns, dragging a freshly killed bison calf.

After cooking and eating the meat, Sits-By-The-Door gets up and tries to continue to her camp, but finds she does not have the strength to walk. The wolf, sensing her difficulty, comes to her. She places a hand on his back, and he seems glad to bear her weight. Many days later, thanks to the Medicine Wolf's support and offerings of food, Sits-By-The-Door makes it back to her people.

When Brings-Down-The-Sun finished the story, he added that because his tribe believed that wolves would help them in times of desperation, the killing of a wolf was taboo. It was very bad luck to shoot at a wolf. As Brings-Down-The-Sun put it, "The Blackfeet never shoot at a wolf, believing them to be good medicine. We have a saying, 'The gun that shoots at a wolf will never again shoot straight.' "

Nearly anywhere in North America, when an Indian heard a wolf howl or when a wolf heard a human voice, the reaction was very likely the same. Each respected the other; they were brothers, kindred spirits.

EUROPEANS IN A NEW WORLD

In 1620, the Pilgrims left England and sailed for the New World, a place that they hoped would be free of the religious, social, and political oppression they had endured in their native land. Soon after landing at Plymouth, they spotted wolves running through the woods. The sight startled them, for wolves had been exterminated in England and no Pilgrim had ever seen or heard a wolf. Once they realized wolves surrounded their new colony, they feared for their lives and for the safety of their livestock.

Two letters written by Pilgrims, reprinted in the book *Letters from New England: The Massachusetts Bay Colony 1629–1638*, clearly convey the feelings of the colonists toward wolves. A minister, in describing the New World, wrote, "Our greatest enemies are our wolves." Another letter, written by a woman, lists the terrible obstacles her family faced as it tried to tame the Massachusetts wilderness. The most frightening aspect was the demonic sound they nightly heard from the woods: "the wolves at midnight howling." To the immigrants, this hated, noxious animal blocked their plan to subdue the New World. This symbol of evil had to be rooted out to make Massachusetts a proper civilization.

Plymouth Colony passed a bill establishing a cash bounty on wolves in 1630. By 1640, the bounty stood at forty shillings per wolf, a payment equivalent to a month's wages for a laborer. A subsequent Massachusetts law, passed in 1644, offered three quarts of wine to any Indian who killed a wolf. Within just a few years of

(continued on page 40)

◀ORIGINAL RANGE
OF GRAY, RED, AND
MEXICAN WOLVES

▪ Gray wolf (*Canis lupus*)
▪ Red wolf (*Canis rufus*)
▪ Mexican wolf (*Canis lupus baileyi*)

Sources: *The Wolves of North America*, by
Stanley Young; L. David Mech, USFWS.

APPROXIMATE RANGE
OF GRAY, RED, AND MEXICAN WOLVES
IN THE 1930s AND EARLY 1940s ▶

▪ Gray wolf (*Canis lupus*)
▪ Red wolf (*Canis rufus*)

This species was considered extinct in the wild by 1980.

▪ Mexican wolf (*Canis lupus baileyi*)

By the early 1940s, only a few stragglers survived in remote parts of Arizona and New Mexico. Extensive wolf control programs instituted in Mexico in the 1950s began to decimate the last viable breeding populations. At the present time, no known Mexican wolves exist in the wild.

Sources: *The Wolves of North America*, by Stanley Young;
"A Perspective on the Taxonomy of Wolves in North America"
by Ronald Nowak, in *Wolves in Canada and Alaska*, ed. by Ludwig Carbyn;
L. David Mech, USFWS; Gary Henry, USFWS.

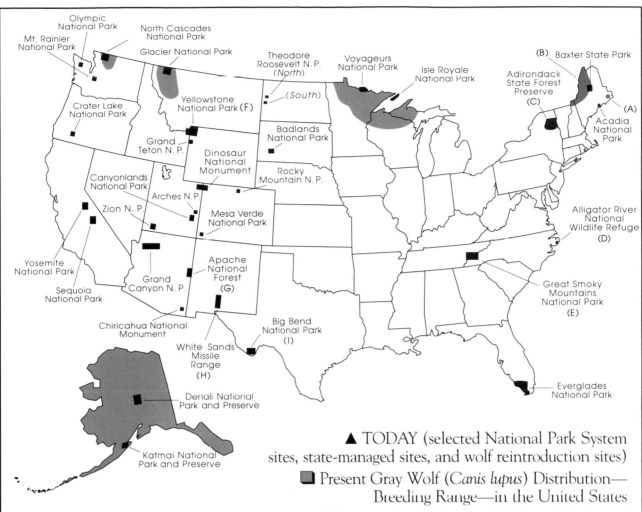

▲ TODAY (selected National Park System sites, state-managed sites, and wolf reintroduction sites)

■ Present Gray Wolf (*Canis lupus*) Distribution— Breeding Range—in the United States

Sources: Steve Fritts, USFWS; L. David Mech, USFWS; *Index to USGS Topographic Map Coverage of National Park System*, Department of the Interior, U.S. Geological Survey.

Wolves are now recolonizing former portions of their North American range, both by natural and assisted means. A subspecies of the gray wolf, the eastern timber wolf (*Canis lupus lycaon*), may eventually be reintroduced into one or more potential sites in northeastern United States: eastern Maine (A), northern New Hampshire and northwestern Maine (B), and the Adirondack State Forest Preserve in northern New York (C). Wolf experts caution that these plans are, at this time, only conceptual. The red wolf (*Canis rufus*) has already been reintroduced into the Alligator River National Wildlife Refuge in North Carolina (D) and into the Great Smoky Mountains National Park (E). Wild-born wolf pups have been produced at both release sites.

Gray wolves (*Canis lupus*) from Canada have migrated into Washington and Montana, establishing breeding populations in both states. Individuals from the Montana wolf population have dispersed into Idaho, and at least one Montana wolf made it to Wyoming but was killed by a hunter just south of Yellowstone National Park. At least ten dispersing wolves from Minnesota and Canada have entered North and South Dakota, but all were shot and killed. In Oregon, particularly the region around Crater Lake National Park, a number of sightings of wolflike animals have been reported, but so far no proof of a wolf population in the state has been documented. Wolves will likely be reintroduced into Yellowstone National Park (F) within the next few years. A U.S. Fish and Wildlife Service study is now evaluating potential sites in Colorado for a future reintroduction program.

The Mexican wolf (*Canis lupus baileyi*), another subspecies of the gray wolf, may be reintroduced into several possible sites in southwestern United States: the Apache National Forest (G) in Arizona, the White Sands Missile Range (H) in New Mexico, and Big Bend National Park (I) in Texas.

See chapter 3, "A Place for Wolves," for more information.

settlement, the colonists in Virginia, Rhode Island, New York, Pennsylvania, New Jersey, and nearly every other settled area set up bounties "For encouragement to destroy the wolves" (as expressed by a 1632 Virginia law). In addition to the bounties, Pennsylvania, in the early 1700s, used taxpayer money to hire professional wolf hunters to track down and kill all the wolves in the colony. As happened to the wolves of England, the wolves of New England and surrounding areas eventually were all destroyed.

In the mid-1800s, the concept of "Manifest Destiny" fueled a surge of human migration across the continent. When white adventurers and settlers reached the Great Plains, they found herds of bison so vast that they had to be measured in number of miles rather than number of individuals. A Kansas pioneer estimated that one bison herd had a length of sixty miles and a width of twenty miles. Closely attending the bison was their main predator, the wolf. The fact that both bison and wolves thrived as part of a well-balanced, highly productive ecosystem escaped notice.

An adult wolf resting on snow. Contrary to the way wolves are depicted in medieval fairy tales, there never has been a documented case of a healthy wild North American wolf attacking and killing a person. In Alaska, I frequently had close encounters with wolves but never felt threatened. Loose dogs are far more of a threat to people than wolves are.

The newcomers found that they could make an extremely good living by killing bison and selling their hides and tongues. An experienced hunter often earned $200 a day, a payment one hundred times the salary of a normal job and three times more than the president of the country received. The number of bison hunters was so great that an 1872 newspaper article reported: "Every ravine is full of hunters and campfires can be seen for miles in every direction." The relentless slaughter of the herds turned out to be a great boon for the wolf packs. The bison hunters left behind most of the meat from the carcasses. The wolves feasted, and their numbers increased dramatically.

Animosity toward wolves caused many bison hunters to shoot them out of spite. Some hunters tanned wolf hides and took them to the fur traders with the bison pelts. A demand for wolf pelts developed and soon a man could get as much as $5 for one in prime condition. Many of the wolf hides ended up in Russia where they adorned the winter uniforms of the czar's soldiers.

As the numbers of bison dwindled, many hunters switched to wolves, taking advantage of the high prices offered for their pelts. Calling themselves "wolfers," these men quickly perfected an efficient method of killing large numbers of wolves: They laced bison carcasses with strychnine.

James Schultz once worked as a wolfer and described his experiences in several issues of *Forest and Stream* magazine published in January 1901. Schultz and three partners set up a base camp on the Missouri River in Montana, ideal territory for wolfers. As one of the men observed, "They's lots o' wolves prowlin' round jest achin' to be poisoned."

Once winter set in, and the wolves were in prime condition, the men went to work. They shot seven bison, ripped open the carcasses, and drenched them with poison, pouring as many as three bottles of strychnine into a single cow. They then gave the wolves a day to find the baits. When the wolfers later checked their stations, sixty-three poisoned wolves lay on the ground. Near the carcasses were scores of dead coyotes and foxes, too worthless to skin or even bother counting.

The wolfers worked hard all winter, shooting and poisoning bison and skinning wolves. By spring, they had a cache of nine hundred prime wolf pelts. A river steamer picked them up, and upon reaching civilization, they received $4,500 for the pelts. People on the steamer and in town treated the wolfers like great heroes for poisoning so many wolves.

Schultz's parties and others like it did their work well. Historian Edward Curnow estimates that the wolfers poisoned as many as one hundred thousand wolves every year in Montana between 1870 and 1877. Men bragged about the number of wolves killed at a single bait. A wolfer named Bill Martin claimed a count of 120 wolves at one poisoned carcass.

Only a handful of the original sixty-five million bison survived the massive slaughter of the late 1800s. The loss of that prey base forced the wolves of the great plains to seek out alternative targets: the cattle and sheep that had replaced the bison.

The Indians hated the white bison hunters and the wolfers. They could not comprehend why a human being would destroy and waste so much. Natives riding the plains saw the countless bison the white man had slaughtered and the vast numbers of dead wolves, coyotes, foxes, bears, and eagles scattered about the poisoned carcasses. Indians wondered if such a people could have souls. Historic reports mention that enraged Indians would attack and kill wolfers for this unforgivable offense against nature.

By the early 1880s, the bison had vanished from the Great Plains, an occurrence that would have seemed unimaginable just a few years earlier. What once had been prime wildlife range became ranchland. Like the Old World wolves centuries earlier, the plains wolves of the New World lost their prey base. To survive, many wolves began targeting the cattle and sheep that had replaced the bison. It was either that or die. By preying on livestock, the wolves incurred the endless wrath of settlers and ranchers who depended on those domestic animals for their livelihood. Thus the stage was set for an all out war: American society versus wolf society.

(continued on page 47)

The Alpha Pair: Who's the Boss?

At the age of thirteen, Susan Bragdon signed up as a volunteer wolf observer at the Washington Park Zoo in Portland, Oregon. Biologist Paul Paquet introduced her to the pack of captive wolves that she would watch and pointed out the alpha male, the leader of the pack. After teaching her how to decipher and record wolf behavior, Paquet left, and Bragdon went to work.

When the biologist later reviewed the young woman's observation notes, he immediately noticed a major mistake. On her forms, she listed the alpha female as the dominant wolf, not the alpha male. Concerned that the new volunteer could make such a significant misjudgment, Paquet went over to the pen. Although he was certain from his observations that the male led the pack, he decided to watch the animals with an open mind. Before long, he came to a startling realization: The alpha female really was the dominant pack member! The expert wolf biologist had been wrong, and the inexperienced teenager was right.

After that incident, Paquet paid close attention to the issue of male and female leadership in wolf packs. Now, after many years of study, he had concluded that, "The majority of wolf packs I've closely observed in captivity and in the wild have been led by a female." His statement represents a radical change in the understanding of wolf pack politics. Traditional dogma states that the alpha male is the dominant wolf, the undisputed leader of the pack. This misinterpretation might have been partially due to an unconscious bias by male wolf researchers, who until recent years, have

conducted the vast majority of wolf studies.

A pattern emerges when biologists analyze the duties, responsibilities, and privileges that commonly characterize the two alpha positions. The alpha male usually takes the initiative in all matters of interpack politics, such as scent marking his pack's territorial boundaries and in chasing away or attacking trespassing wolves. He normally is the only male to breed, partly because he blocks any mating attempts by lower-ranking males. The alpha male is often the central figure in pack ceremonial and bonding activities, such as howling sessions and prehunt rallies. In this role, he appears to motivate the other pack members to work together as a cooperative unit. The lead wolf in a hunt and during an attack on prey is usually, but not always, the alpha male.

The alpha female's primary responsibility involves directing the pack's reproduction efforts. She normally prohibits all other females from breeding and selects the male who will father her pups. That usually will be the alpha male, but if she chooses, she might reject him and breed with another male. Because she ultimately controls the maternity and the paternity of the pups, she governs the future genetic makeup of the pack far more than the alpha male.

The alpha female also picks the denning site—the single most important decision of the year for the pack. Biologist Diane Boyd once told me, "If the alpha female selects a poor den site or dens in an area of low prey density, the entire year's reproduction may fail,

Facing page: *The mother wolf digging out the den. Her choice of a denning site is perhaps the single most important decision made by the pack during the year.* Above: *The mother wolf playing with her six-week-old pups. During the mating season and pup-rearing season, the alpha female is the most dominant wolf in the pack.*

based solely on her choice of den site." After the alpha female gives birth, the survival of the pups depends primarily on her mothering skills. Other pack members assist her with the pups, but if she is a poor mother, the litter likely will not survive to adulthood. Throughout the breeding season and extended period of pup rearing, the alpha female clearly dominates pack activities.

During the rest of the year, the pack travels and hunts as a unit. In her studies of wolves in the Glacier National Park area in Montana, Diane Boyd frequently sees female wolves leading hunts. I often saw the East Fork female in Alaska doing the same thing: She was the one who killed the caribou calf and shared it with her mate, the limping alpha male.

Many biologists I spoke with used the phrase "shared leadership" when they described pack government, meaning the alpha animals divide pack leadership into components that one or the other directs. This shared leadership is not necessarily a fifty-fifty split. In some packs, the alpha female controls most activities and thus might be considered the dominant pack member. Other packs have alpha males that oversee the majority of functions. It would be rare for one wolf to dominate every facet of pack life.

Perhaps the greatest similarity between wolves and humans is the great potential for variation in individual personalities and temperaments within each species. As happens with people who function as a group or a team, the dominant figure in a pack could be either a male or a female. The leader of a pack, if there is just one leader, will be the wolf that has the best leadership and decision-making skills. Convergent evolution apparently has brought wolf society and human society to the same advanced point: Leadership in group activities can be a shared duty, or it can be directed by a single individual of either sex.

Above: This alpha male was the brother of the alpha female. Perhaps because of a natural instinct to avoid inbreeding, the alpha female bred with the beta male. The alpha male helped to raise the pups as if they were his own. Left: Mother wolf watching her pups. Erik Zimen, a German wolf researcher, has said ". . . the alpha female is actually the most prominent member of the pack. She is the real leader despite all the attention afforded the alpha male. . . ." However, most experts think the alpha male and female share leadership duties.

An East Fork wolf pauses for a rest while out hunting. Adolph Murie said of the East Fork wolves, "It was an inexhaustible thrill to watch the wolves simply because they typify the wilderness so completely."

THE NATIONAL PARKS AND THE WAR ON WOLVES

A PATCH OF WHITE, ABOUT A MILE ACROSS THE TUNDRA, catches my eye. Looking through my binoculars, I see that it is a wolf. Its coloration—bright white fur—matches the markings of the East Fork alpha female. Hoping to watch her hunt, I set up my forty-five-power scope.

As I focus on her, I notice a second wolf stretched out fifty feet away. Looking over the nearby area, I find a total of five wolves. Except for the white female, all the other pack members are light gray in color. Soon they all get up and trot off to the east. I then see that the largest of the gray wolves has a pronounced limp in his front left leg. He holds his paw in the air and rarely puts his full weight on it. This is my old friend, the alpha male. He and the white female are almost certainly the parents of the other wolves.

As the pack travels, the limping male falls behind. At times he rushes forward on three legs and momentarily catches up. When he drops several hundred yards behind, the other pack members halt and patiently wait for him to reach them.

The wolves frequently stop to socialize. The white female, the mother, invariably is the center of attention. The younger wolves repeatedly come up to her and touch noses or roll on the ground under her. She, in turn, gives most of her attention to the limping male. The pack is in high spirits, like a group of kids on its way to play ball in a vacant lot.

The evening moves on and the pack rests. Suddenly all five wolves simultaneously sense or see something. Jumping up, they run off in close formation, shoulder to shoulder, to the west. The excitement causes the old male to ignore the pain in his crippled foot; he runs on all fours for the first time. One of the younger wolves runs faster than the others; it breaks away from the pack and sprints ahead.

Above: *Grizzly chasing an East Fork wolf from a caribou carcass.*
Right: *Four members of the East Fork Pack, including the alpha female and beta male.*

The lead wolf is ten lengths ahead of the others when something new appears in the margin of my scope. The pack is chasing a grizzly bear! The bear is just a few lengths ahead of the first wolf, who is now seventy feet ahead of the pack. Surging forward, the lead wolf closes the gap to five feet. The grizzly looks back over its shoulder.

As both animals run, they momentarily lock eyes and communicate with each other in a way that no human can decipher. Whatever passes between them, it causes the wolf to end the chase. The bear continues on a short distance, stops, glances back, then calmly begins feeding on grass.

The wolf who led the charge trots back to its companions, and the pack immediately leaps into exuberant play. They wag tails, touch noses, playfully nip each other, run side by side, and roll on the ground. The wolf who played tag with the bear is the focus of the play. From a human perspective, it looks like a joyous congratulatory celebration. For fifteen minutes, the wolves give uninhibited expression to their emotions. Several hundred yards away, the grizzly eats its dinner in quiet dignity.

This evening I watch the East Fork Pack for two hours. I think, What does it means to belong to a pack? The East Fork wolves are teaching me something that I can never learn from any book or research paper. They embody and demonstrate the joy of companionship that wolves experience by belonging to a pack.

∾

YELLOWSTONE AND THE IDEA OF THE NATIONAL PARK

As the great herds of bison were being slaughtered in the late nineteenth century, some of the European immigrants and their descendants reexamined their perceptions of wilderness and its relationship to civilization. The philosophy of Henry David Thoreau, which once seemed so radical, now found favor with increasing numbers of Americans. Thoreau, in his writings, spoke of the importance of having an "oases of wildness in the desert of our civilization." In an 1851 lecture at the Concord Lyceum, he proclaimed that, "ever I am leaving the city more and more, and withdrawing into the wilderness." At the conclusion of his talk, Thoreau summed up his attitude toward nature by saying, "In Wildness is the preservation of the World."

In 1858, Thoreau wrote an article for the popular magazine, *Atlantic Monthly*, about his experiences in the Maine wilderness. He used the piece to issue a challenge to his fellow citizens: "Why should not we . . . have our national preserves . . . in which the bear and panther, and some even of the hunter race, may still exist, and not be 'civilized off the face of the earth' . . . not for idle sport or food, but for inspiration and our own true recreation?"

Thoreau's arguments convinced many Americans that there could be great value in the preservation of wilderness. A debate on this new philosophy took place around a campfire in a remote part of Wyoming, on the evening of September 19, 1870. As Nathaniel Langford reported, that night he and other members of the Washburn-Doane Yellowstone Expedition discussed development plans for the spectacular wilderness they had just explored. Most of the party members spoke of their intent to file claims on the most valuable features of the landscape so they could profit from tourists who would soon flock to the area.

One man disagreed with this plan to commercialize Yellowstone. Cornelius Hedges, later Montana's U.S. District Attorney and president of the territorial historical society, argued that Yellowstone "ought to be set apart as a great National Park." This vision for Yellowstone deeply impressed Langford, an influential politician, writer, and lecturer.

Langford, on returning to civilization, mounted a public relations campaign for the proposed national park. Due to Langford

and many others who enlisted in the cause, Congress established Yellowstone National Park on March 1, 1872, as a place "reserved and withdrawn from settlement, occupancy, or sale . . . and set apart as a public park or pleasuring ground for the benefit and enjoyment of the people." The Secretary of the Interior was ordered to "provide for the preservation . . . of all timber, mineral deposits, natural curiosities, or wonders within said park . . . in their natural condition," and to prevent "wanton destruction of fish and game."

In all the official pronouncements about Yellowstone, something remained unsaid. The attitude toward wilderness may have changed, but public opinion on wolves and other predators remained the same: Preservation did not apply to the wolf—the species needed to be exterminated!

Yellowstone National Park's 2.2 million acres lie in what are now the states of Wyoming, Montana, and Idaho. Despite the protection that park status appeared to confer on game animals, commercial hunters, throughout the 1870s, came into the preserve to shoot game animals and sell the meat and hides. General W. E. Strong, who visited Yellowstone in 1875, reported that professional hunters had slaughtered thousands of game animals in the park. The park boundary, an imaginary line on government maps, posed no barrier to the poachers. Little could be done to stop the destruction of wildlife. Congress had not yet appropriated any money to staff Yellowstone, so the first park superintendent, Nathaniel Langford, served as a volunteer and had no paid staff. Market hunters, taking advantage of initial regulations that allowed limited subsistence hunting in the park, could claim that all their kills were done on a subsistence basis.

In the 1877 superintendent's annual report, the section on wildlife stated that illegal hunters killed game in the park and poisoned the carcasses for "wolf or wolverine bait." Superintendent Philetus Norris, in his 1880 annual report, commented that wolves and coyotes "were once exceedingly numerous in all portions of the park, but the value of their hides and their easy slaughter with strychnine-poisoned carcasses of animals have nearly led to their extermination by 1880." Norris's remarks about wolves and coyotes express a legal concern with poaching, not regret at the killing of predators. Within just eight years of the park's creation, the Yellowstone wolves were close to extinction.

Civilian management of Yellowstone, mainly due to lack of

Along with grizzlies, elk, deer, and bison, the wolf was a critical component of the original ecosystem in Yellowstone.

Top: *Philetus Norris, Yellowstone's second superintendent, found that professional hunters had poisoned nearly all of the park's original wolf population by 1880. (Photo courtesy of Yellowstone National Park.) Above: A photograph of the first detachment of soldiers stationed in Yellowstone, 1886. In a 1907 booklet on official rules and regulations issued to soldiers stationed in Yellowstone, the following order appears: "Scouts and noncommissioned officers in charge of stations throughout the park are authorized and directed to kill mountain lions, coyotes, and timber wolves." (Photo courtesy of Yellowstone National Park.) Right: Yellowstone: The world's first national park, established in 1872.*

Left: The U.S. Army and the National Park Service felt it was their mission to exterminate all of the wolves in Yellowstone. Below: The Yellowstone wolves were killed because they were falsely believed to be "a decided menace to the herds of elk, deer, mountain sheep and antelope," as stated in a 1915 annual park report.

funding, could not stop the flagrant poaching. In 1886 the Secretary of the Interior asked the U.S. Army to administer the park. For the next thirty-two years the army ran Yellowstone. A statement that typifies the army's attitude toward predators appeared in Captain F.A. Boutelle's 1889 superintendent's annual report: "The carnivora of the park have, along with other animal, increased until, I believe, something should be done for their extermination."

Federal laws governing Yellowstone's wildlife became strengthened in 1894 when Congress passed the Lacey Act. The act's stated function was "to protect the birds and animals in Yellowstone National Park." Among the activities forbidden were "all hunting or the killing . . . of any wild animal or bird." For the first time, substantial fines could be levied against poachers. But, that protection of "any wild animal" was probably not intended to include the wolf, given the contemporary attitude toward wolves. In any event, the original Yellowstone wolf population was nearly gone by this date.

The army, despite the clear wording of the law, decided that the Lacey Act didn't really apply to all the park animals. They felt some exceptions needed to be made. Concerned over the number of coyotes in Yellowstone, the army, in the 1890s, mounted a campaign to shoot, trap, and poison them. Using the wolfers' technique, the military put out poison bait throughout the park. By the time of the 1914 annual report, the army had been destroying coyotes for years. That year's report listed 155 coyotes killed by the men. In addition, nineteen mountain lions had been run down by government-owned hounds and killed.

As the elk, deer, and other game animals recovered due to the protection provided by the army and the Lacey Act, people began seeing a few surviving or colonizing wolves. At

Left: *Tower Junction Area. A large portion of Yellowstone's original wolf population was concentrated in this north central section of the park.* Above: *An unknown park ranger on patrol in Yellowstone. Yellowstone records indicate that at least 136 wolves were destroyed in the park during the years 1914 to 1926. (Photo courtesy of Yellowstone National Park.)*

57

Above: *Yellowstone park rangers about to leave Mammoth Hot Springs for a patrol, 1922. By 1935, the U.S. Army and the National Park Service had killed at least 121 mountain lions and 4,352 coyotes within Yellowstone. (Photo courtesy of Yellowstone National Park.)* Right: *National Park Service records indicate that at least eighty of the 136 wolves killed in Yellowstone were pups.*

least one pack of ten was spotted in 1914. The army, alarmed at the resurgence of wolves, began targeting them along with coyotes and mountain lions. Soldiers killed seven wolves along the park's northern boundary in December 1914. The Yellowstone superintendent clearly stated his attitude toward wolves: "They are very destructive of game and efforts will be made to kill them."

The 1915 annual report continues along the same lines. It describes wolves as "a decided menace to the herds of elk, deer, mountain sheep and antelope." After mentioning that his men had shot several wolves, the superintendent said that "an effort will be made this coming winter to capture or kill" the rest of the wolves.

In the report dated 1916, the superintendent stated that "two special rangers were employed . . . for the purpose of exterminating carnivorous animals in the park." The men shot or trapped eighty-three coyotes, twelve wolves, and four mountain lions. Other Yellowstone employees killed an additional ninety-seven coyotes that year.

Congress created the National Park Service (NPS) in August 1916, to manage the national parks in a professional manner. The administrative change over from the U.S. Army to the NPS did not deter the wolf extermination program. If anything, it escalated to a higher level.

A legal basis for the control actions came from the 1916 Con-

gressional act that established the NPS. The act gave the Secretary of the Interior authority to order "the destruction of such animals . . . as may be detrimental to the use of any of said parks." Rangers in the big wildlife parks knew that tourists came to their areas to see the game. Wolves and other predators became factors "detrimental" to visitors' chances of seeing that game.

The 1918 annual report described the first year of coyote and wolf management in Yellowstone by the new federal agency:

These animals have done much damage to other game, and for that reason much pains have been taken to hunt them down and trap them. Two expert hunters were employed as scouts during the winter and spent most of their time hunting and trapping. Steve Elkins, the famous guide and mountain lion hunter, was also employed for several weeks with his pack of lion hounds hunting lions, wolves, and coyotes.

The report added that two U.S. Biological Survey men worked the park, destroying wolves. By the end of the season the body counts totaled thirty-six wolves, 190 coyotes, and twenty-three mountain lions.

Some conservation groups criticized the Yellowstone wolf control program, but the NPS stood by its position. "It is evident

Yellowstone park rangers killed many litters of wolf pups in dens along Tower and Hellroaring creeks in the 1920s. In April of 1922, the superintendent's monthly report states "Wolf dens located first week of April between Blacktail and Hellroaring, and adult female killed and 10 pups captured alive." Those pups were briefly put on display at park headquarters then killed. (Photo courtesy of Yellowstone National Park.)

that the work of controlling these animals must be vigorously prosecuted by the most effective means available," wrote the superintendent in 1922, "whether or not this meets with the approval of certain game conservationists."

Outside influences strongly affected the policy and actions of the NPS. Livestock owners living near park boundaries worried that park-based predators would cross the border and kill their animals. During the 1928 superintendents' conference, NPS director Stephen Mather spoke about this anxiety of the livestock industry:

> In Yellowstone, if Mr. Albright [the current superintendent] didn't kill off his 200 to 300 coyotes a year it might result in being the developing ground for the coyotes and wolves spreading out over the country and the cattle or sheep men getting much greater losses than they ordinarily would.

Hunting-oriented associations also demanded predator control within national parks. Many of these groups were powerful national organizations that had worked to get parks such as Yellowstone, Glacier, and McKinley established. They felt they had a legitimate right to influence the management of the parks. The superintendent of Yellowstone, during the 1932 superintendents' conference, summed up the NPS response to this pressure:

> We have always assumed . . . that the elk and the deer and the antelope were the type of animals the park was for. We have had the support of the game associations only on the basis that the parks would act as reservoirs for the game and the increase would overflow and form legitimate hunting. If we change that policy and say there is to be no killing, coyotes will increase to balance the increase of the deer and elk, there will be no hunting and we would have no support whatsoever from the sportsmen's associations. . . . To me a herd of antelope and deer is more valuable than a herd of coyotes.

The NPS archives indicate that early rangers, due to their good animal-bad animal orientation, were all too willing to accommodate the interests of the livestock and hunting groups.

In 1975, the NPS hired biologist John Weaver to search Yellowstone archives for records on the wolf control program. Weaver documented a minimum of 136 wolves shot, trapped, and poisoned during the period of most intensive control, 1914 to 1926. Prior to the government-sponsored extermination program against the Yellowstone wolf, poachers and wolfers poisoned a large but unknown number of local wolves.

Yellowstone park ranger E. Burket, 1922. According to the superintendent's monthly reports, twenty-six wolves were killed in the park during 1922. At least sixteen of those wolves were pups. Four years later, Yellowstone park ranger M. P. Skinner wrote in his Yellowstone Nature Book, ". . . every fall after the tourists leave, certain of our more experienced rangers are detailed to hunt mountain lions, wolves, and coyotes, although no hunting is done in summer for fear of stray bullets." (Photo courtesy of Yellowstone National Park.)

Above: Yellowstone park rangers Ted Ogston and Samuel Woodring, posing by coyotes shot in the park, 1927. (Photo courtesy of Yellowstone National Park.) Right: McDonald Creek, Glacier National Park. As in Yellowstone, a "campaign of extermination" was carried out against the wolves of Glacier.

Weaver's report, *The Wolves of Yellowstone*, pointed out that eighty of the 136 wolves killed were pups. As in other parts of the West, the most efficient method of exterminating wolves was to find dens, destroy the pups, then trap or shoot the returning parents. Dens near Tower Falls, Hellroaring Creek, and Blacktail Deer Creek were discovered, and the residing litters killed. In a typical report from May 1922, the Yellowstone superintendent noted the discovery of a wolf family at a den on Specimen Ridge and the subsequent destruction of both parents and six pups. Another report mentioned that an employee sealed up an active den, trapping the pups underground. On at least one occasion, dynamite was dropped into a den filled with pups.

In 1926, Yellowstone phased out its wolf control program. This was done, not for humanitarian reasons, but simply because wolves no longer had a significant presence in the park. A 1928 monthly report proudly mentioned that, "There have been no wolf signs reported this season." In later years, sporadic accounts and rumors of wolf sightings came into park headquarters, but no resident packs or active dens could be documented. Except for a few rare stragglers, wolves had been eliminated from Yellowstone as the 1920s drew to a close.

GLACIER NATIONAL PARK

Glacier National Park, a one-million-acre kingdom of rugged mountainous terrain in northern Montana, came into existence in 1910. The attitudes of park administrators toward wolves, coyotes, and mountain lions, which dominated in Yellowstone, also prevailed in Glacier. As early as 1914, park employees placed poisoned bait throughout Glacier. Hounds ran down mountain lions and kept them at bay until they could be shot. The 1915 Superintendent's Annual Report mentioned use of traps and poison for predator control.

Top: *Coyotes killed on the border of Glacier National Park by Roderick Huston of Belton, Montana. Wolves, coyotes, and mountain lions were shot, trapped, and poisoned inside the park as well as outside. (Photo courtesy of Glacier National Park.)*

Middle: *A deer feeding station at Lake McDonald Ranger Station, Glacier National Park, January 1935. Park rangers fed deer and bighorn sheep during the winters in the 1920s and 1930s, in an attempt to prevent mass starvation. The killing off of wolves and other predators in Glacier likely contributed to an unnaturally high population of game species. (Photo courtesy of Glacier National Park.)*

Bottom: *Frank Liebig, a forest ranger for the national forest that later became Glacier National Park. In this photo, taken prior to 1910, Liebig is posing next to skins of animals he had killed near Lake McDonald. At this time forest rangers had embarked on an extermination campaign against wolves, coyotes, mountain lions, and other predators on national forest lands. (Photo courtesy of Glacier National Park.)*

Facing page: *Park ranger Dan Doody worked in Glacier National Park until 1916. Like other early rangers, Doody's responsibilities included killing predatory animals within the park. (Photo courtesy of Glacier National Park.)*

The most detailed account of predator control in Glacier National Park is recorded in the 1918 Annual Report of the Director of the National Park Service (NPS). In describing "the campaign of extermination that is being inaugurated against the predatory animals in the park," the report notes that the NPS entered into an agreement with the U.S. Bureau of Biological Survey (USBS), later renamed the U.S. Fish and Wildlife Service, under which the USBS would train and oversee predator control agents in Glacier and the NPS would pay the agents' salary. The two men hired for the jobs established trap lines throughout Glacier for the purpose of "systematically clearing the park of predatory animals."

Wolfers and trappers had wiped out most of the local packs before the establishment of the park. James Schultz wrote of a group of wolfers who boasted of killing hundreds of wolves during the 1870s, in an area that later formed the eastern boundary of Glacier. Due to the low wolf population during the early years of the park, most of the animals killed by government traps and poisoned baits were coyotes and lions.

A NPS historical study conducted by biologist Francis Singer found records of twenty-nine wolves shot or trapped in the Glacier area between 1910 and 1975. Singer emphasizes that his tabulation is only a partial list of wolf kills. The NPS and USBS poisoning campaigns killed an unknown number of additional park wolves.

By the late 1920s, the native wolf population in Glacier was considered extinct. As in Yellowstone, sightings of wolves trickled in over the years. Most likely, the animals were wolves dispersing from Canadian packs to the north, who never settled in the park. Park Service records indicate no packs were permanently established in Glacier after the 1920s.

THE WAR AGAINST THE WOLF

The treatment afforded wolves inside Yellowstone and Glacier national parks was just part of the same pattern and attitude that dominated the rest of the United States in the late nineteenth and early twentieth centuries. During that era, government officials, farmers, ranchers, and even early conservationists all agreed that the wolf "problem" had to be "controlled."

Like disease, droughts, storms, rustling, poor husbandry, and unstable market prices, wolves represented a tangible menace to the livelihood of livestock raisers. But the wolves were more easily confronted and conquered than the other threats. Ranchers reacted to the wolf situation by pressuring county, state, and territorial governments to post bounties on the thieving predators. Colorado established a wolf bounty in 1869, Wyoming passed bounty laws in 1875, and Montana followed suit in 1883. Other western

states and territories joined the bandwagon.

By 1914, government bounties paid out on wolves and other predators exceeded one million dollars per year. Edward Curnow, while researching his thesis, *The History of the Eradication of the Wolf in Montana,* tabulated that Montana paid out bounties on 80,730 wolves during the period 1883–1914. According to figures compiled by federal predator control agents Albert Day and Almer Nelson, 35,455 wolves were turned in for bounties in Wyoming between 1895 and 1915.

Wolf bounties had to be regularly increased. For example, the original Montana rate was one dollar for every wolf. Thousands of wolves were killed, but the goal of extermination had not been achieved, so, to offer a greater incentive, Montana raised its bounty every few years; by 1911 the going rate was fifteen dollars per wolf.

Ranching associations posted private wolf bounties that supplemented and often greatly exceeded the government rates. Rewards of fifty dollars per wolf were paid in parts of Montana, and one Colorado association, located near Rocky Mountain National Park, offered $175. Anyone who killed a wolf received bounties from the local livestock association, the state, and in many cases, the county. Such lucrative rewards were hard to ignore. During this period a cowboy's monthly salary averaged twenty-five dollars.

The war against the wolf then escalated into one of the earliest attempts at germ warfare. In 1905, Montana passed a bill requiring the state veterinarian to capture wolves, infect them with mange, then turn them lose in hopes that they would spread the highly contagious disease to other pack members. Private citizens could collect fifteen dollars from the state for every wolf they infected. Despite the possibility that mange could be transmitted to other species of game and livestock, the program was carried out.

Ranchers who grazed livestock on the newly created national forests demanded that the U.S. Forest Service protect their animals from wolves. In 1907, forest rangers received a manual entitled *Directions for the Destruction of Wolves and Coyotes,* which instructed them in techniques of "trapping, poisoning, and hunting wolves and finding the dens of young." A supply of steel traps came with the manual, as well as direct orders to immediately implement a wolf destruction program. That year, forest rangers killed 1,810 wolves on thirty-nine national forests in the western states.

Even with the steep bounties, germ-warfare project, and U.S. Forest Service's antiwolf program, a few wolves still survived. The prevailing opinion was that the number of wolves couldn't just be reduced, the species had to be completely eradicated from all land, public and private. Ranchers and hunting organizations insisted that the federal government conduct an organized campaign to rid the West of wolves once and for all. Congress bowed to the pressure, and in 1915 ordered the U.S. Biological Survey (USBS) to oversee and coordinate a national wolf control program.

The USBS's mission was clear to all who worked for the agency. J. Stokley Ligon, the official who directed the program in Arizona and New Mexico, promised that "the gray wolf will be exterminated throughout the west." While admitting that "the gray wolf tribe will die hard," he guaranteed that they would not stop "until the last animal is taken." The official campaign slogan said it all: "Bring Them In Regardless of How."

The federal government hired a staff of three hundred full-time hunters and trappers to carry out the extermination program. The men spread out over the western states and used guns, traps,

(continued on page 75)

Left: Private bounties on wolves offered by livestock associations ranged as high as $175. At that time, most cowboys earned only about $25 a month. Inset: A romanticized illustration from the cover of a 1955 issue of Field and Stream *magazine of aerial predator control agents saving an Alaskan caribou from a wolf pack. (Copyright © by* Field and Stream *magazine, courtesy of Colorado State University Library.)*

Above: A Wyoming wolf hunter, Coyote Smith, with a freshly killed wolf. (Photo courtesy of Wyoming State Museum.) Left: For the first time in the history of the planet, one species made a deliberate, organized attempt to exterminate a fellow species.

Duel in Colorado: Bill Caywood versus the Wolf

The men who signed on as predator control agents with the U.S. Bureau of Biological Survey became mythic, larger-than-life figures to their contemporaries in the old West. No agent better fit this description than Bill Caywood. He was judged to be the toughest, smartest, and most experienced wolf killer by his fellow trappers and by his boss, Stanley Young. During his long career, Caywood killed many legendary outlaw wolves. The death of one of these renegades, a shaggy-coated wolf named Rags the Digger, had a pronounced effect on the trapper.

Ranchers in northwestern Colorado demanded that Young, the Biological Survey supervisor for all predator control in Colorado, send Caywood to handle the case of Rags the Digger. No other man would be acceptable. At the time, Caywood was over fifty and had three decades of wolf-trapping experience. In the words of a Colorado cattleman, "He knows more about wolves than they know about themselves."

Rags, deemed by stockmen to be the toughest, craftiest, and most experienced wolf in the Colorado and Utah region, never stayed in one location for long. He ranged over a two-state kingdom that covered ten thousand square miles. This master wolf, for fourteen years, had survived endless trapping and poisoning attempts. No human could touch him.

The wolf had plenty of reasons to hate people. His first mate had died in a steel trap set for him. He later found another mate and had a litter of pups with her. While Rags was out hunting for his family, a trapper found the den and killed the female and entire litter. Wolfers, men who hunted wolves for bounty, believed that the psychological effects of finding his slaughtered family pushed Rags to new heights of vindictiveness against humanity. Destruction of livestock served as his preferred method of retribution.

Legend grew around the wolf. Stories were told that Rags loved to demonstrate his innate superiority over people. Whenever he found a wolf trap hidden in the soil he would carefully dig it up, then flip it out of its hole so that it could be plainly seen by all who passed by. He could accomplish the whole operation without tripping the delicate spring on the deadly trap. This flagrant display of contempt enraged ranchers. Banding together, they brought in the greatest wolf hunter who ever lived to challenge this outlaw wolf to mortal combat.

Caywood, a big man with leathery, weatherbeaten skin, drew on his vast experience to set out masterfully concealed traps in places where Rags might travel. These traps, buried a fraction of an inch below the surface, were undetectable to man or beast. Looking at his handiwork, Caywood felt the pride of accomplishment that only an artist or master craftsman can experience. Throughout his long career, the government man had never failed "to get his wolf"; Rags would be no exception.

Then the day came when Caywood found one of his traps dug out by Rags and disdainfully deposited on the trail. The trapper had never seen anything like this. Caywood readily deciphered a message: "He's dared me to come at him if ever a wolf's dared a man." This defiant challenge only made Caywood try harder. From then on, it became a personal duel between the man and wolf that could only end with the death of one or the other. Despite his best efforts, Caywood continued to come up short. Local ranchers began kidding him about his failure. "You've met your match," one cattleman told him, "Rags is your equal, Bill. He's outguessing you." Caywood taciturnly replied, "I'm not sayin' when I'll get him, but I will."

The fruitless attempts to trap Rags taught Caywood a few things about his adversary. The government agent's thoughts dwelled on the wolf's namesake habit of digging up traps. Then one day, the way to catch Rags came to Caywood. He rode out, found a likely place that Rags would travel through, and set a trap in a deliberately amateurish manner. No wolf, especially one as experienced as Rags, could miss it. Behind the initial trap, Caywood set two additional ones, muttering, "Here's a surprise for you, old timer," as he worked.

The renegade was hunting sheep in Utah at the time. On returning to Colorado, Rags trotted right up to the trap that Caywood had so sloppily set. With more contempt than usual, Rags began digging up the deadly steel mechanism. To uncover the far side, the wolf had to step over the trap. The instant he put his paw on the ground, a second, well-hidden trap sprang shut around his foot! Caywood had used the obvious trap as a decoy; the real traps were placed just behind it, where the wolf was sure to step if he tried to dig out the decoy. As Rags struggled to free himself, a third trap leaped up and grabbed another foot. Brilliantly, Caywood had used Rags' own arrogance to settle the score. Although two traps held the wolf, his personal duel with Caywood was far from over.

When Caywood checked his traps the next morning, he saw that two had been sprung and dragged off. He knew he had caught the wolf, but experience taught him not to celebrate victory until

Above: *Cattle in Rio Blanco County, Colorado, the former home range of the wolf Rags the Digger.* Right: *Despite the fact that their job was to exterminate wolves, many federal predator control agents developed a great respect for their adversaries. (Photo courtesy of North Dakota Game and Fish Department.)*

The accompanying story of Caywood's epic duel with Rags is based on interviews he gave to two writers, Arthur Carhart and Stanley Young. Carhart and Young published the earliest version of the story in their 1929 book, The Last Stand of the Pack. *Additional information from Caywood appeared in Carhart's article "World Champion Wolfer" (*Outdoor Life, *September 1939) and in Young's 1946 book,* The Wolf in North American History.

Like Rags the Digger, this wolf was caught in two steel traps. (Photo by J. Stokely Ligon from The Wolf of the Southwest, *David E. Brown, editor.)*

he had the dead animal in hand. Following the injured wolf's trail on horseback was easy. The heavy chain and drag hook attached to the two traps left a trail the newest of greenhorns could follow. As he pursued the wolf, Caywood couldn't help admiring Rags's courage and determination. The iron hook frequently had caught on branches and the trapper could see where Rags had yanked the chain until it pulled free. Caywood cringed when he thought of the intense pain the violent jerking would have created in the wounds, still encased in sharp steel.

Coming to the top of a one-hundred-foot cliff, Caywood lost the trail. Looking over the edge, he spotted Rags's tracks at the bottom of the cliff. The wolf had simply jumped to the bottom and continued on, still dragging the traps, chain, and hook. As he circled around the cliff, the predator control agent wondered if anything could stop this wolf's valiant attempt to gain freedom.

The climax to the pursuit came a few minutes later. Directly ahead, Caywood spotted Rags in a narrow arroyo. At first the wolf continued on, then he stopped and stared back at his nemesis. Drawing his rifle, Caywood dismounted and walked toward his

quarry. Wolf and man stared at each other, seventy-five yards apart, both knowing the duel was about to end. Then Rags did something unexpected—he started walking toward Caywood. The dragging traps slowed him, but he moved steadily forward, straight for the trapper.

Caywood, never having been stalked by a wolf, froze. He was dumbfounded that a wolf with such serious injuries would still have any fight left. With regret at having to destroy such an admirable spirit, Caywood raised his rifle, aimed at Rags head and pulled the trigger. Nothing happened. He tried firing again but the gun jammed a second time. As he fumbled with the rifle, Rags continued to close the gap between them. When he was thirty feet away, Caywood couldn't resist looking up at him. The wolf had an expression on his face that, despite Caywood's decades of experience with wolves, was completely unreadable. Suddenly the trapper remembered how a rancher had warned him about Rags: "Whatever you do, Bill, don't let that old devil catch you on foot without a gun . . . he'd make mincemeat of you in forty seconds." Was the wolf coming to kill him or to acknowledge, as one wolf might concede to another wolf, that his enemy had beaten him in a fair fight? Mesmerized by the force of the wolf's personality, Caywood stood still with the useless rifle hanging at his side.

Something, perhaps the sound of the clanking metal, broke the spell and Caywood tried the gun again, but it once more failed. Rags now was fifteen feet away and still coming. When they were ten feet apart, a revelation suddenly struck Caywood. Could the wolf be coming to him so that he could remove the traps from the animal's paws? This possibility shook the hardened trapper to his very core. Rags now was almost close enough to touch. Caywood had no idea if the wolf would leap at him and tear out his throat or simply hold out the entrapped paws. Frozen in place, the master predator control agent waited for the wolf to play out his hand. Then, from deep inside Caywood, a lifetime of experience in wolf killing took over his body, severing it from the befuddled mind that had rendered that body helpless. He raised the rifle one last time, aimed at Rags's chest and pulled the trigger. The gun fired and the wolf, just eight feet away, slumped to the ground.

Caywood instantly knew the bullet had gone through Rags's heart. Holding the gun, he stood silently as the life drained out of his courageous adversary. Waves of regret passed through him; he didn't know if he had done the right thing. As he tried to sort out his feelings, Rags opened his eyes and looked up at Caywood.

Now thoroughly spooked, the trapper stared in disbelief as the wolf painfully struggled to his feet and, still dragging the two traps, stumbled forward, gasping for air. Again incapable of any action, Caywood watched the wolf apparition inch closer and closer. Then, for the first time, Rags's indomitable spirit failed him and his lifeless body collapsed to the ground. The wolf's nose landed a fraction of an inch from Caywood's foot. "You poor old devil!" the trapper cried as he bent down and stroked the wolf's fur, "You poor, lonely old murdering devil!"

A rancher once asked Caywood if he got a kick out of killing a wolf. The old trapper replied:

"Oh, yes and no. I've just got a lot of love and respect for the gray wolf. He's a real fellow, the big gray is. Lots of brains. I feel sorry for him. It's his way of livin'. He don't know better. And I feel sorry every time I see one of those big fellows thrashin' around in a trap bellowin' bloody murder. Guess I'm too much a part of this outdoors to hold any grudge against animals."

The same rancher wondered what would become of Caywood in the years to come: "Ever since I can remember you've been around here wagin' war on the wolves. What you goin' to do when they are all gone?" The question proved to be prophetic, for Caywood himself later killed the last wolves in his part of Colorado. After thinking hard about the matter, Caywood told the cattleman:

"Don't know. Guess I'll dry up and blow away like a tumbleweed. I couldn't no more go into town and live, settle down in some store or something like that, than I could fly on horseback. Guess it's in my blood, this outdoors. My daddy and mother started me out on this career. They come across the plains in an ox-drawn prairie schooner when I was only three years old. I've lived in the outdoors, near the ragged edge of what we call civilization, ever since. It's meat and drink to me. No chance for me reformin' and settlin' down so long as I can navigate on horseback."

Government predator control agents like Bill Caywood believed they were doing honest, honorable work in exterminating the wolf from the western United States. These predator control agents were master outdoorsmen who used their hard-earned knowledge of wildlife and trapping skills to carry out government policy as best they could.

Nearly always, when expressing their feelings about the way the West was becoming "civilized," they spoke of their respect for the wolf and the way it had lived free and wild on the open range. The passing of the wolf meant that the time of the wolf hunters had also passed. These tough men had made the West "safe" for civilization but realized that they could never fit into this new order, nor would they want to. In the end, they admitted that they admired the old outlaw wolves far more than they admired the human society that had ordered their destruction.

Left: By the 1950s, only a few hundred wolves lived in the lower forty-eight states, a tiny fraction of the original population of two million. Below left: Michael Lavy, a professional wolfer, in September 1902. He boasted of killing 242 wolves and coyotes for the five-dollar bounty offered by the state of Montana. (Photo by Evelyn Cameron, courtesy of R. H. Renn.) Right: Lone Running Wolf, a Blackfeet Indian, admired wolves so much he named himself after the species and always drew the symbol of a wolf next to his signature, below. (Photo courtesy of Montana Historical Society.)

poison, and dog packs to kill wolves. The dogs not only found and ran down wolves, they also located dens. To the government predator controllers, "denning" was the ultimate in efficiency. A whole litter of pups could be destroyed in moments. Sometimes they accomplished this by pouring fuel down the entrance and setting the den on fire.

At many dens, one pup would be temporarily spared. The predator control agent would chain the terrified pup to a tree and then hide near the den so he could shoot any pack members who returned to rescue the pup. Ironically, the wolves' loyal commitment to their pups enabled the agents to destroy the entire pack. Traits that would have been admired in people only made the wolves easier to kill.

Agency reports and newsletters give a glimpse of the attitude of the times. One employee, held up as a role model to others, was called "one of our veteran poisoners." Unsubtle references were made to men who had been fired because they did not kill enough wolves. In 1923, the USBS bragged that it had scattered poisoned bait over thirteen million acres of public land in Arizona. A history of the agency, written in 1929 by Jenks Cameron, lists a total of 419,447 predatory animals killed in twenty-one western states from 1915 to 1928. Writer Charles Bowden, after looking over the agency's archives, commented that the "records are a bit like a history of the Jews as Hitler might have written it."

The wolves, already decimated from loss of habitat and wild prey, could not survive such an obsessive, all-out government-run crusade. By the late 1930s, only a few stragglers survived in the western states. Relentless campaigns were mounted to destroy the last of these defiant loners. It took years to track down some individual outlaw wolves, but every one was finally killed. When an occasional wolf from Canada or Mexico strayed across the border, it was mercilessly pursued and slaughtered.

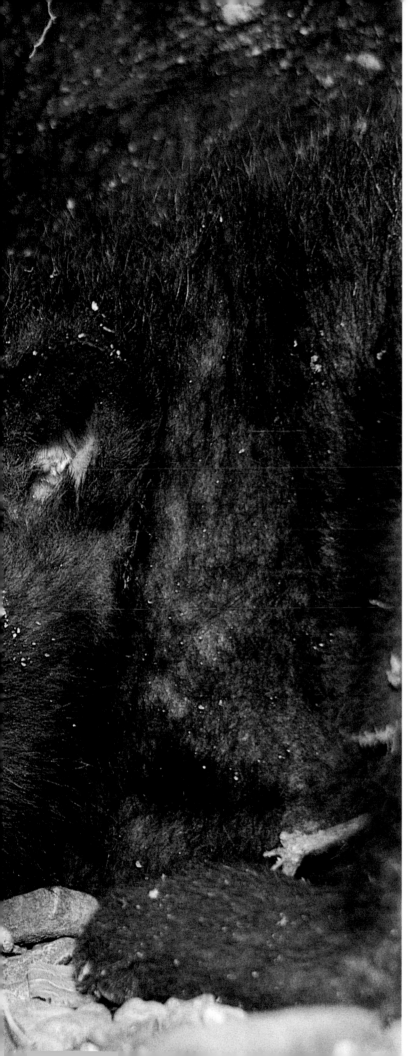

The Biological Survey even sent agents into Mexico to teach local ranchers how to poison wolves. The agency also suggested that a wolf-proof fence be installed along the United States—Mexican border to guard "against infestation from Mexico."

No one knows the number of wolves destroyed during our war on the species. Naturalist Ernest Thompson Seton calculated that the wolf population of the lower forty-eight states was originally two million. By the 1950s, except for isolated populations of a few hundred wolves in the Upper Midwest, the gray wolf had been exterminated in the forty-eight states. From two million to a few hundred: The war against the wolf was one of the most successful programs ever carried out by the federal government.

Barry Holstun Lopez, in his thoughtful book, *Of Wolves and Men*, analyses this brutal crusade to eliminate wolves from the West:

> A nation that wanted beef had to control wolf predation—had to kill wolves—there was no way around that—but it didn't have to, as it did, kill every last wolf. . . .
>
> . . . the motive for wiping out wolves (as opposed to controlling them) proceeded from misunderstanding, from illusions of what constituted sport, from strident attachment to private property, from ignorance and irrational hatred. But the scope, the casual irresponsibility, and the cruelty of wolf killing is something else. I do not think it comes from some base, atavistic urge, though that may be a part of it. I think it is that we simply do not understand our place in the universe and have not the courage to admit it.

What must the Indians have thought of this mindless destruction of their brother tribe? No doubt, Native Americans saw in wolves a reflection of the way they themselves had been persecuted. Like the wolf, most tribes had their original land and traditional game stolen away. Indians and wolves, once

The technique of "denning," killing pups in the den, destroyed the wolves' ability to reproduce.

Above: *Three federal agencies waged war on the wolf in the lower forty-eight states: the U.S. Forest Service, the U.S. Bureau of Biological Survey, and the National Park Service. The war against the wolf was one of the most successful programs ever carried out by the U.S. government.* Left: *Dick Brown, a Montana wolfer. Note the pile of wolf traps to left of Brown and wolf hides piled up on his right. (Photo by Evelyn Cameron, courtesy of Montana Historical Society.)*

Top right: *During the 1950s and 1960s, at the lowest ebb of the wolf population in the lower forty-eight states, Minnesota was the only state with a viable wolf population. Wolves survived in northern Minnesota not because they were given any protection or sanctuary, but because the vast wilderness tracts in that portion of the state made wolf extermination too difficult. During this period, to encourage destruction of wolves, Minnesota offered bounties of $35 for adult wolves and $25 for pups. Right: A Minnesota wolf hunter in the 1950s. (Photos courtesy of the Minnesota DNR.)*

Above: As wolf biologist Steve Fritts observed, "Possibly no animal has been so misunderstood, feared, hated and persecuted throughout history as the wolf." (Photo courtesy of the National Archives.) Right: A young boy proudly stands in front of fifteen wolf hides in Baker, Montana, 1934. (Photo courtesy of Montana Historical Society.) Facing page: Predator control agents with the U.S. Biological Survey spread poison bait on millions of acres of public lands, hoping to exterminate the wolf. Along with the wolves, large numbers of bears, foxes, eagles, and other predators and scavengers died from the indiscriminate poisoning campaign.

Right: *Taking whatever time was needed, federal predator control agents trapped or poisoned the last of the lone wolves in the western states. Above: Inevitably, when a famous wolf was finally killed, its body would be propped up and photographed. Such grotesque pictures were later passed from generation to generation as a testament to victory in the war against the wolf. (Photo courtesy of North Dakota Game and Fish Department.)*

Below: *Hounds such as these were used by government predator control agents and private bounty hunters to run down adult wolves and to locate active wolf dens. (Photo from Mrs. Elizabeth Roberts, courtesy of Mrs. Ted Pope and the North Dakota Game and Fish Department.)* Right: *Senator Ben Nighthorse Campbell, a descendant of the Northern Cheyenne Indians, wrote, "May there never come a time when a person alone in the wild country could not hear the lonely, yet comforting, cry of the wolf."*

brothers in the hunt, became brothers in exile.

James Schultz, in his book, *Why Gone Those Times*, recorded a speech made by a Blackfeet medicine man named Morning Eagle about Chief Wolf and Chief Bear, the spirit entities who watched over the wolf and bear tribes. Morning Eagle had witnessed the plight of the plains wolf and guessed that his tribe would suffer a similar fate. Speaking to his fellow Blackfeet, Morning Eagle tried to reassure them with these words:

> But even if in these late days the old gods, Chief Wolf, Chief Bear and others, no longer come and talk with us in person, we know that they still roam the earth, that they live in some far part of it which the white men have not yet found and desecrated, and we have the assurance that they still visit us in the spirit, unseen and unheard except as they appear to us in our dreams. And we know that they still heed our prayers and intercede for us with the sun, ruler of all, for his mercy and aid.

An East Fork pack member. R. D. Shaw, chief archaeologist for the Alaska Department of Natural Resources, wrote in a May 1991 article for Alaska magazine, "If societies are judged by their systems of order, justice, land rights and family, the kingdom of the wolf is one of the most sophisticated. Few creatures, two legged or four, honor a hierarchical system with such respect, teach and nurture their young with such diligence, defend their territories with such passion, and hunt and fight for survival with such dogged ferocity."

A PLACE FOR WOLVES

THE EAST FORK ALPHA MALE IS THE TOUGHEST ANIMAL I've ever known. For at least seven years, his left front paw has been so badly swollen that he can hardly use it. He lost part of that foot, most likely in a steel trap set just outside the park boundary where it is legal to take wolves.

I often see him chase caribou. Knowing that he can't catch them if he gives in to his disability, he runs on his maimed foot and somehow sprints at speeds close to that of much younger, sure-footed wolves. He endures what must be an extremely painful ordeal and often gets his prey. After a chase, he lies on the tundra and licks his injured, bleeding foot, sometimes for an hour, before he can go on.

One summer day, as the limping alpha male is on a solo hunt, he finds a young bull moose. The bull outweighs him by four hundred pounds, but the alpha takes the big animal on by himself, challenging the moose to a fight to the death. Over the next thirty-six hours, he attacks the moose at least fourteen separate times. The moose fights back, stomping and kicking his attacker. The wolf's bad paw is hit during the counterattack and bleeds profusely.

Each attack weakens the moose. Near the end of the drawn-out battle, he wades out into a swift river channel. Jumping into the water, the wolf swims to his opponent. As they fight, the moose holds the alpha under water and nearly drowns him. The wolf slips away to rest, then comes back for one last round. By this point, the wounds on the bull have taken their toll. Weak from loss of blood, the moose can't fight back any longer, and the wolf finishes him off. After the moose dies, other East Fork pack members arrive and feed alongside their leader.

The limping wolf pays a heavy price for his hard-fought victory. His injuries will slow him down considerably in the weeks ahead. Within a month he will disappear, and I will never see him again. The beta male, a wolf who is also a skilled hunter, will take over the alpha position. This male, like nearly all the other East Fork wolves, almost certainly was fathered by the limping wolf.

∽

Top left: *The limping alpha male of the East Fork Pack, feeding on a caribou carcass.* Bottom left: *An East Fork wolf feeding on a Dall ram killed earlier in the day by the pack. When wolf researcher L. David Mech examined the carcass, he found that the ram had been suffering from severe arthritis, a disability that would have prevented the ram from running or climbing as well as healthier sheep in his band.* Above: *The wolf on the right became the new alpha male of the East Fork Pack after the limping wolf died. He is almost certainly the son of the old alpha. Note the submissive pose of the other pack member traveling with the alpha male.*

CHANGING ATTITUDES TOWARD WOLVES

The idea of park rangers shooting, trapping, and poisoning wolves and other predators in national parks seems unimaginable in today's ecology-minded American society. Yet it once happened on a wide scale. In addition to taking place in Yellowstone, Glacier, and McKinley/Denali, predator control also occurred in many other national parks: Rocky Mountain, Grand Canyon, Wind Cave, Mesa Verde, Mount Rainier, Yosemite, Sequoia, Crater Lake, and Zion—as well as on other federal, state, and territorial government lands and on private land. For the wolf, no safe haven existed in the United States or its territories.

In hindsight, it is easy to condemn the actions of federal employees who carried out the wolf control programs for the National Park Service, U.S. Forest Service, and U.S. Biological Survey/U.S. Fish and Wildlife Service. But these people believed that they were doing the right thing, and the public supported them. Very few conservation groups or individuals ever questioned the government policy on wolves. Wolf extermination was the American way of life.

An evolution of attitudes toward wolves and other predators began to be apparent in the National Park Service (NPS), and in the larger society, beginning in the 1930s. A 1933 statement that became Park Service policy read in part: "No native predator shall be destroyed on account of its normal utilization of any other park animal, excepting if that animal is in immediate danger of extermination." Despite the plain wording, some rangers used loose interpretations of the phrase "danger of extermination" to justify continuations of predator control programs in Yellowstone and McKinley national parks.

Into this controversy stepped Adolph Murie, a young biologist who, more than any other individual, changed the way park managers perceived wolves and other predators. The NPS funded a study of Yellowstone coyotes in 1937 and picked Murie to conduct the research. He arrived at a time when many local rangers felt coyote control was still necessary. As he started his project, Murie discovered that at least 4,352 coyotes had been killed in Yellowstone from 1907 to 1935. His assignment was to study scientifically the coyote and its food sources. The findings would determine whether coyote control would continue in Yellowstone.

After two years of extensive field work, Murie wrote a report entitled *Ecology of the Coyote in the Yellowstone*. Based on an analysis of over five thousand droppings, he found that Yellowstone coyotes fed mostly on rodents and carrion. Their effect on game species was negligible. According to Murie, overcrowded habitat was the limiting factor for park game animals, not predation. Concluding that the coyote should be considered a desirable member of the Yellowstone wildlife assembly, Murie advised against any continuation of control programs. (More recently, NPS biologists have found that harsh winter weather was the primary controlling factor on animal populations in the park. In either case, coyotes were not an important factor in population fluctuations of game species.)

Murie's sound, reasoned research on the Yellowstone coyotes led, in 1939, to a new assignment: the study of wolves and Dall sheep in Mount McKinley National Park. After walking over 1,700 miles in the sheep hills, collecting the skulls of scores of sheep killed by wolves, and watching wolves hunt sheep, Murie wrote his 1944 book, *The Wolves of Mount McKinley*. His research documented that wolves tended to kill the youngest, oldest, and sickest individuals in a prey population. Because they cull out unfit members, Murie wrote that the wolves played a beneficial role "in the maintenance or improvement of the species."

As he watched the packs attempt to kill sheep, Murie saw a pattern develop. Sheep that stayed near steep cliffs could escape the wolves by bounding up a rock wall. Any sheep that moved away from rough terrain were much more likely to be caught. "As an evolutionary force," Murie wrote, "the wolf may function most effectively by causing the sheep to dwell in a rocky habitat." By restricting them to that rocky country, the wolves limited the population increase of sheep. That limitation kept them in rough balance with the carrying capacity of their range and worked to prevent the wild population upswings and inevitable crashes that occurred in areas without predators.

Murie's scientific analysis of wolves caused the NPS to terminate the McKinley wolf control program in 1943. During the next few years, a well-organized campaign by antiwolf interests demanded that the program be reinstated. In 1945, Congress considered a bill that would have required the NPS to severely control wolves and other predators in McKinley. Attempting to avoid legally mandated predator control programs, the agency reluctantly agreed to a voluntary resumption of wolf control in the park. The killing of wolves in McKinley, as an official Park Service policy, finally ended in 1952.

If Murie provided the scientific foundation for our modern

(continued on page 96)

Above: *The pioneer research that Adolph Murie did on the East Fork wolves and other wolves in Mount McKinley/Denali National Park provided the scientific basis for the National Park Service's modern understanding of the role of predators in national parks.* Right: *During the early days of his career, Aldo Leopold would have gladly killed every wolf he saw. Later, after shooting a wolf and watching it die, Leopold became convinced that he had been an "accessory in an ecological murder."*

The Wolves of Isle Royale National Park

The gray wolf population of the lower forty-eight states reached its lowest ebb during the 1950s. Except for a few stragglers, wolves had been exterminated in all but the upper midwestern states. Those states, Wisconsin, Michigan, and Minnesota, still offered bounties on wolves. The last known wolf in Wisconsin died in 1957. By the early 1960s, wolf packs in the Upper Peninsula of Michigan had declined to a few scattered nonbreeding individuals. Minnesota, the last of the lower forty-eight states with a viable wolf population, offered $35 wolf bounties until 1965.

This bleak picture was somewhat ameliorated by events that unfolded on a remote Michigan island in Lake Superior. During the winter of 1949, extremely cold weather created an ice bridge that connected the mainland of Ontario with Isle Royale, a 210-square-mile island national park, fifteen miles off the Canadian shore. A pack of Ontario wolves, perhaps just an alpha pair, used that ice bridge to reach the U.S. island. The wolves, discovering that the high density of moose and lack of human persecution would make the area a perfect home, set up a territory.

Realizing the opportunity for research, Durward Allen of Purdue University fashioned a long-term plan to study wolves and moose on the island. The project, now in its thirty-fifth year, became, in Allen's words, "the greatest of all experiments in predator-prey relationships." Dr. Allen selected a graduate student named L. David Mech to conduct the first in a long series of research projects. Mech began his field work in 1959 and published the results in his 1966 book, *The Wolves of Isle Royale*.

During the initial years of research, Mech, Allen, and other biologists documented a classic example of the natural equilibrium that develops between a predator and its prey. The researchers discovered that the moose killed by the wolves were very young, old, or unhealthy. No kills occurred in the one- to five-year-old age classes, the animals of prime age. The moose population, which in previous decades had alternately risen to levels of great overpopulation, then crashed due to overbrowsing and malnutrition, became far more stabilized due to the governing effect of wolf predation. The number of cow moose having twins, a sure sign of population vigor, jumped from 6 to 38 percent after the wolves arrived. The wolves clearly had stimulated moose reproduction.

During its second decade, the Isle Royale study uncovered a significant new aspect of wolf-moose relationships. As Durward Allen reported in his 1979 book, *The Wolves of Minong* (Minong, the Ojibway name for the island, means "place of blueberries"),

the wolves began preying on increasing numbers of prime-age moose, contradicting the well-accepted studies that wolves primarily kill just the young, old, weak, and sick.

As Allen and the other biologists studied their data, they found an explanation for the seeming contradiction. During the first ten years of the project, winter weather and snow levels were relatively mild. That trend dramatically changed in 1969 when snowfall in the park built up to particularly deep levels. Two out of the next three winters also had heavy snowfall. The moose, despite their long legs, could not efficiently travel through the deep snow and soon began to suffer from malnutrition.

For the wolves, the weakened moose became easy targets. Animals that normally could have fought off a pack now could be easily dispatched. The good hunting lasted far beyond the times of deep snow. The cumulative effects of three harsh winters created long-lasting weaknesses in many moose, making them vulnerable targets for years to come. With these new findings, the study showed how weather conditions could cause prime-age animals to develop vulnerabilities that gave wolves a decided edge.

As expressed by Allen, "the wolves entered a period of unprecedented prosperity" due to the availability of vulnerable prey. The number of packs increased, and pup production soared. By 1980, the island contained fifty wolves or one wolf per five square miles, a density twice the level experts thought possible.

That prosperity was short-lived. The moose population, greatly reduced by a decade of intense pressure from wolves, no longer offered an abundance of prey. Between 1980 and 1982, the wolf population crashed from fifty to fourteen. During that two-year period, the island's packs experienced a social upheaval that caused wolves to kill other wolves in territorial warfare. As these events occurred, lowered predation rates, recovering vegetation and mild winter weather caused the moose population to rebound. By 1984, the increasing prey density enabled the wolf population to climb to twenty-four, a level close to the long-term average for the island.

Rolf Peterson, a professor at Michigan Technological University, succeeded Durward Allen as the director of the Isle Royale study in 1975. Peterson and his fellow researchers studied the data from the period 1969 to 1984 and found that it revealed a long-term cycle in the relationship between wolves and moose. Due to the lag time in feedback between moose, wolves, climatic conditions, and edible vegetation, the biologists concluded that a cycle averaging thirty-eight years characterized the island's moose-wolf ecosystem. Within that cycle, substantial fluctuations could occur in both moose and wolf populations, but like a pendulum, the system eventually reverses direction when the fluctuations reach their peak. Thanks to the dramatic events taking place on Isle Royale, science was beginning to understand how ecosystems, the most complex entities known to humanity, function and cycle over long periods of time.

The next chapter in the Isle Royale wolf-moose story is now being written. An unexpected drop in wolf numbers and pup production began in 1988 and continues to this day. In early 1993, only twelve wolves could be found on the island, the lowest count since the study began.

Wolf pack traveling on snow, Isle Royale National Park. (Photo by Rolf Peterson.)

This ominous decline could easily wipe out the entire Isle Royale wolf population. Due to the seriousness of the situation, the National Park Service, for the first time, allowed researchers to capture, exam, and radio collar wolves in the park. This phase of the research will try to find the cause of the decline. Possible explanations include food scarcity, disease, and inbreeding problems.

The healthy condition of the captured wolves and the high density of moose on the island imply that food shortage is an unlikely limiting factor. Testing of wolf blood samples found that several animals had antibodies to Lyme disease, canine hepatitis, and canine parvovirus. Parvovirus is a highly contagious virus that killed many dogs in nearby shoreline communities in the early 1980s. No dogs are allowed on Isle Royale, but rangers often find evidence that visitors have illegally brought pets onto the island. Rolf Peterson believes that canine parvovirus has probably run its course at Isle Royale but likely was a very important factor in the early 1980s.

The effects of excessive inbreeding may prove to be the most significant problem. DNA testing of the captured wolves showed that they all are very closely related and probably all descended from the original founding pair. On an island, lack of new genetic material will eventually create an "inbreeding depression" that can result in low reproduction, high pup mortality, and lowered resistance to disease. As Wisconsin nature writer Jeff Rennicke puts it, the wolves may be "falling victim to the very isolation that once made Isle Royale seem such a safe haven."

Because of the National Park Service policy of noninterference with natural processes, it is critically important to determine the primary cause of the Isle Royale wolf decline. If inbreeding, a natu-

ral process, turns out to be the root cause of the problem, the Park Service may decide to allow the situation to run its course. A detailed study of the decline of the Isle Royale wolves will help biologists understand how genetic isolation affects wildlife populations. That information could then be used to help prevent such a situation from developing in other national parks, areas that, like Isle Royale, have become isolated "biological islands." In coming years, this genetic stagnation may become the most critical problem in many national parks.

If this natural process does cause the Isle Royale wolves to die off, the park managers would have several options to consider. Under completely natural conditions, an ice bridge eventually would allow new wolves to cross from Ontario to the island. Current development along the Lake Superior shoreline, however, presents a barrier that may stop wolves from ever again making that migration. Because of that unnatural obstruction, a program to restock Isle Royale with a new pack might be considered.

The story of the Isle Royale wolves demonstrates the value of using national parks as outdoor research laboratories. Only through long-term studies of wildlife populations in completely wild ecosystems can we truly understand how nature functions. Durward Allen expressed the excitement biologists feel when they study the pristine ecosystem of a place like Isle Royale National Park: "It is one of those continuous searches into the unknown that has no foreseeable end."

The Mexican Wolf: On the Brink of Extinction

The smallest and southernmost of the gray wolf subspecies, the Mexican wolf (known to science as *Canis lupus baileyi* and locally called *lobo*) originally lived in mountainous terrain in Arizona, New Mexico, west Texas, and Mexico. This is the type of wolf that Aldo Leopold shot, watched die, and later regretted killing. The Mexican wolf is extinct in the wild in the United States, and probably is extinct in the wild in Mexico as well. If any remnant populations still endure in Mexico, they have little chance of surviving due to rural development and human persecution.

The Mexican wolf is the most endangered wolf subspecies and one of the rarest animals in North America. In early 1992, the known population of pure-blooded Mexican wolves totaled just thirty-eight animals. By the beginning of 1993, their numbers had climbed to fifty-three. Those animals, all liv-

ing in captivity, are descended from four wild wolves captured in Mexico in the 1970s. Intensive breeding programs, located at fourteen zoos and captive facilities in the United States and Mexico, are working toward increasing that perilously low population.

Once the captive population reaches a minimum of eighty to one hundred animals, the U.S. Fish and Wildlife Service proposes to experimentally reintroduce Mexican wolves at one or two of five sites currently under consideration: White Sands Missile Range (adjacent to the White Sands National Monument) in New Mexico and four locations in southeastern Arizona. In late 1992, the Arizona Game and Fish Department began a feasibility study for a possible reintroduction at Blue Range Primitive Area, a 150,000-acre site in the Apache National Forest. Due to the Arizona Game and Fish study, the Blue Range area is the

most likely site for a wolf reintroduction in Arizona. The earliest possible date for an Arizona or New Mexico wolf release would be 1995 or 1996.

Wolf advocates in Texas, including retired National Park Service chief scientist Roland Wauer, suggest releasing Mexican wolves into that state's Big Bend National Park. Rangers at Big Bend are now evaluating the park as a potential reintroduction site. The Mexican Wolf Coalition of Texas is conducting a successful public education and lobbying effort directed toward bringing wolves back into the state. Governor Ann Richards has given her "full support" to reintroduction efforts in Texas.

Although Mexican wolf reintroduction is controversial, the public strongly supports the concept. For example, a 1990 public opinion poll sponsored by the Arizona Game and Fish Department found that 77 percent

Left: *A pair of Mexican wolves living at the Rio Grande Zoo, Albuquerque, New Mexico. The Mexican wolf, a subspecies of the gray wolf, is thought to be extinct in the wild, but breeding programs such as the one at the Rio Grande Zoo have saved the subspecies from extinction. In a few years, descendants from this pair and other captive Mexican wolves may be used in reintroduction projects in the southwestern states.*

of Arizona residents would like to have wolves restored to their state.

Due to effective outreach by a conservation group called Preserve Arizona's Wolves, both the Arizona Cattle Growers' Association and the Arizona Wool Producers Association have stated that if certain conditions were met, they would not oppose a wolf reintroduction program. Defenders of Wildlife, the organization that raised money to reimburse ranchers in Montana for livestock lost to wolves, has established a similar fund for southwestern ranchers, The Mexican Wolf Compensation Fund.

This cooperation between ranchers and conservation groups is key to rescuing the Mexican wolf from the brink of extinction and restoring it to its historic range. Soon, the howl of the wild *lobo* may again be heard in the Southwest.

The Eastern Timber Wolf: A Return to Maine, New Hampshire, and New York?

When Europeans began colonizing North America, the eastern timber wolf ranged from what is now Quebec south to the Appalachian Mountains. This subspecies of the gray wolf (*Canis lupus lycaon*) was eventually exterminated from most of its former territory.

In 1992, the U.S. Fish and Wildlife Service published a revision of its *Recovery Plan for the Eastern Timber Wolf*. The plan discusses the possibility of wolf reintroduction projects in Maine (eastern and northwestern sections of the state, including Baxter State Park), New Hampshire (the extreme northern end of the state), and New York (Adirondack State Forest Preserve).

Due to limitations in funding and personnel, and political complications, the Fish and Wildlife Service is currently giving low priority to these possible reintroductions. That priority level could change if a well-organized campaign, like the one calling for wolf reintroduction in Yellowstone, lobbied to restore the timber wolf to its ancestral home in the northeastern United States.

The Wolf Recolonization of Washington State

Washington State is now going through the beginning stages of wolf recolonization. In the early 1980s, a number of sightings of wolflike animals occurred in the Cascade Mountains. These individuals were likely dispersing wolves from southern British Columbia. In 1990, biologists confirmed the presence of wolves in North Cascades National Park.

The following year, based on reported wolf sightings, the Washington Department of Wildlife estimated that five packs of wolves lived in the state. By early 1993, the agency's count rose to seven packs. Wolves are now believed to live south of Mount Saint Helens (not far from the Oregon border), and wolf reports are coming in from the Mount Rainier National Park area.

The rugged terrain of Washington's mountain ranges makes documentation of wolf populations difficult, so other packs may exist in the state. Any sightings of wolflike animals in Washington should be called in to a hot line (800-722-4095) established to compile reports of wolf activity. Washington residents who would like to get involved with this exciting recovery process should get in touch with Wolf Haven, a nonprofit group based in Tenino. Their address is listed on page 119.

understanding of the role of wolves, Aldo Leopold supplied the philosophical support for a new appreciation of the value of wolves. Leopold's understanding of wolves underwent a dramatic evolution in his lifetime. The changes in his attitude toward wolves foreshadowed a coming seismic shift in public opinion on wolves and other predators.

Leopold began his career in 1909 as a forest ranger with the U.S. Forest Service, working first in Arizona, then in New Mexico. Convinced that wolves and other predators had to be destroyed, he campaigned to get federal and state funding for predator control programs. Leopold called wolves "vermin" and "varmints" as he preached the antiwolf gospel to any who would listen. In a 1920 speech to the National Game Conference in New York, he proudly announced that in just three years, predator control agents had killed 90 percent of the wolves in New Mexico. A later passage in his speech shows that his position on complete eradication of wolves was consistent with the times: "It is going to take patience and money to catch the last wolf . . . but the last one must be caught."

In later years, Leopold became one of the greatest thinkers and writers in the ecology movement and a founder of the Wilderness Society. His most famous book, *A Sand County Almanac*, published in 1949, contains a brief essay entitled "Thinking Like a Mountain." He begins the piece by describing a wolf howl and the possible meanings it carries to the deer, the coyote, the hunter, and the cowman. But the howl also conveys, "a deeper meaning, known only to the mountain itself. Only the mountain has lived long enough to listen objectively to the howl of a wolf."

Leopold reveals the experience that changed his thinking about wolves. As he and a companion ate lunch during a Forest Service patrol, they saw a wolf family—an adult and six pups—come out into an opening and begin to play:

> In those days we had never heard of passing up a chance to kill a wolf. In a second we were pumping lead into the pack. . . . When our rifles were empty, the old wolf was down, and a pup was dragging a leg into impassable slide-rocks.
>
> We reached the old wolf in time to watch a fierce green fire dying in her eyes. I realized then, and have known ever since, that there was something new to me in those eyes—something known only to her and to the mountain. I was young then, and full of trigger-itch; I thought that because fewer wolves meant more deer, that no wolves would mean hunters' paradise. But after seeing the green fire die, I sensed that neither the wolf nor the mountain agreed with such a view.

For Leopold, "thinking like a mountain" meant seeing nature as a whole interdependent system. Destruction of one part invariably pulled other parts out of balance. Like Saint Paul's conversion on the road to Damascus, Leopold's experience of seeing "the fierce green fire" in the eyes of the wolf became a pivotal event in his life. He now sought to think like a mountain and to pass on that enlightened view to others. In his original foreword to *A Sand County Almanac*, Leopold acknowledged his involvement in federal predator control programs and his later realization and regret that he had been an "accessory in an ecological murder."

Along with Murie and Leopold, many other writers and researchers have helped to document and explain the basic principle of ecology, that every element in nature, including wolves, is connected and interrelated. L. David Mech, a biologist with the U.S. Fish and Wildlife Service, carries on in Murie's tradition. For over thirty years, Mech has conducted scores of research projects on wild wolves. He has trained generations of graduate students who now are in charge of their own wolf research projects. Mech has contributed more to our factual knowledge of wolves than any other person in history. In addition, he played a major role in founding the International Wolf Center in Ely, Minnesota, a nonprofit organization dedicated to educating people about wolves.

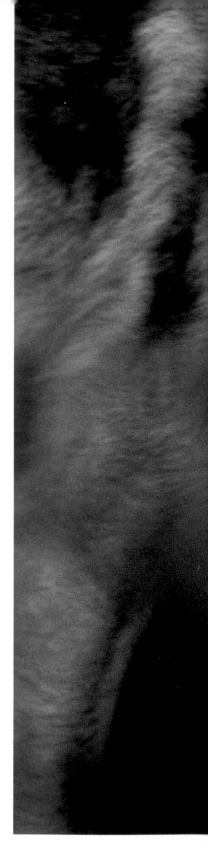

Photo of an alpha male wolf, Katmai National Park, taken by Rollie Ostermick. This male and his pack allowed Rollie to photograph them at close range in the mid 1970s. In 1978 this shot was used on the cover of Barry Holstun Lopez's book Of Wolves and Men. *Shortly before the book was published, the alpha male and ten of his fellow pack members were killed by aerial poachers inside the park boundary. (Photo by Rollie Ostermick.)*

In his 1978 book, *Of Wolves and Men*, Barry Holstun Lopez wrote of the many and passionate ways humans have perceived the wolf. Lopez's brilliant analysis of those perceptions has never been equaled. As Leopold did, Lopez has deeply influenced the way we perceive wolves.

Due to the work and writings of Murie, Leopold, Mech, Lopez, and others, many people now see the wolf as an animal we should respect and preserve. Within the NPS, rangers universally view past wolf control programs as ecological blunders that disrupted long-established natural processes in national parks. Thanks to the 1973 Endangered Species Act, federal law now protects wolves in the lower forty-eight states. The wolf is classified as endangered in all the lower states except Minnesota, where it is listed as threatened. Alaska's population of wolves, approximately six to seven thousand, is not endangered. The penalty for killing a wolf is a fine of $50,000 and up to one year in jail.

Many federal and state agencies and private groups are working to restore wolves to their original range, an action mandated by the Endangered Species Act. Wolves have already recolonized Glacier National Park but may need some assistance in getting back to Yellowstone.

THE RETURN OF WOLVES TO GLACIER NATIONAL PARK

On November 10, 1985, an event of profound importance took place in Montana. During that day a pack of twelve wolves, known as the Magic pack, slipped over the Canadian border and took up residence in Glacier National Park. The wolf recolonization of Glacier was made possible by the protection British Columbia granted wolves, from 1967 to 1987, in the region immediately north of the park. That protection enabled the Canadian wolf population to build up and disperse into Montana.

The alpha female of the Magic Pack dug out a den the following spring and gave birth to five pups. That litter, the first born in the western United States in over fifty years, marked the start of a promising new era in wolf history. In the words of Clifford Martinka, a veteran National Park Service (NPS) biologist at Glacier, "I think this is the biggest thing that has happened here since the creation of the park itself."

Descendants of the original Magic Pack wolves later realigned into four packs. The North Camas Pack and South Camas Pack both live in Glacier, while the Spruce Creek Pack controls a territory that lies partially in Glacier and partially in British Columbia. A fourth group, the Headwaters Pack, lives entirely in Canada but ranges within twenty miles of the Glacier boundary.

During the 1991 season, membership in the four packs totaled twenty-seven. That figure represented a 21 percent drop from the 1990 level of thirty-four wolves, a decrease due to heavy human-caused mortality in the Headwaters Pack. In early 1991, that pack had ten adult members; by late spring only one adult could be located, the alpha female. She had given birth to a litter and was struggling to raise them by herself.

Four members of the Headwaters Pack were found dead in early March. Autopsies determined that poison had killed them. A fifth pack member died in the same area; she also was presumed poisoned. An avalanche killed a sixth wolf. Three other Headwa-

Left: *Kintla Lake, Glacier National Park, the new home range of the Canadian wolves who moved south and recolonized northwest Montana in 1985.* Below: *The Headwaters Pack, based near the northern boundary of Glacier National Park, had nearly all their member poisoned in early 1991. The only known survivor, the alpha female (the wolf on the right), gave birth to a litter of pups that spring and managed to raise two to adulthood. One of those yearlings is seen traveling with the alpha female in this aerial photo taken in February 1992.*

ters wolves disappeared during this period, and wolf biologist Diane Boyd suspects that they also had been poisoned. The alpha female, the only known adult survivor, raised two pups that summer, keeping the Headwaters pack intact as a social unit. Her success at raising two pups without the help of her mate or any other pack members was an incredible accomplishment.

By early 1993, due to high pup survival in the 1992 season, the wolf population in the study area had increased to about forty animals. In addition, wolves born into the four local packs have dispersed into other parts of Montana and Idaho and are establishing packs in those areas.

The University of Montana Wolf Ecology Project, with the support of the NPS, has done an outstanding job in documenting the return of wolves to the Glacier ecosystem and studying the impacts of the restored wolf population on the local prey species. Professor Robert Ream of the University of Montana School of Forestry has directed the Wolf Ecology Project since it began in 1972. The principle field biologists have been Diane Boyd and Mike Fairchild, but many other researchers and volunteers have contributed to the project.

Boyd, who lives in a remote cabin within the wolf study area, typifies the many dedicated wolf researchers whom I had met in Alaska and Montana. She arrived in the area in 1979 to study wolves and coyotes for a master's degree at the University of Montana, just as reports of wolf activity along the international border first became known. The veteran researcher is now in her fifteenth year of studying the Glacier wolf recovery process. Because funding for the Wolf Ecology Project is often inadequate, she does much of her work on a volunteer basis. During those periods, scraping together a meager existence by working as a seasonal lookout in a nearby firetower and selling her artwork, she devoted all her free time to continuing her wolf research.

Although she downplays it, Boyd's life as a wolf researcher has had its dangerous moments. One day, as we talked about her work,

Top left: *British Columbian conservation officer Pat Holder examining four members of the Headwaters Pack killed by poison. The pack's alpha male is second from the right. (Photo by Diane Boyd.)* Above: *A photo of Mojave, the alpha female of the North Camas Pack. Mojave has been the matriarch of the Glacier wolf population since 1987, the year she became the breeding female of her pack. (Photo by Diane Boyd.)* Top right: *Wolf 8756, daughter of Mojave and alpha female of the South Camas Pack. This is the wolf Diane Boyd saved from the grizzly bear. (Photo by Diane Boyd.)* Right: *Diane Boyd has lived along the edge of Glacier National Park since 1979 studying wolves in that area and in adjacent parts of Canada.* Facing page: *Ten members of the North Camas Pack, including Mojave, resting in the snow after a hunt, Glacier National Park.*

she told me the story of the grizzly bear and the wolf. She and Kurt Aluzas, a coworker, had caught a female wolf, placed a radio collar on her, and were waiting for the tranquilizing drug to wear off. Hearing a twig snap, Boyd looked up and saw a grizzly heading straight for the unconscious wolf. She yelled at the four-hundred-pound bear and clapped her hands. The sudden sounds startled the bear, causing it to stop and look around.

Thinking quickly, Boyd told Aluzas to get their jeep, parked a few hundred yards away. Now alone with the grizzly and unconscious wolf, Boyd slowly walked toward the wolf. The bear, seeing her as a threat to its intended meal, moved toward her. When the grizzly got to within twenty-five yards, it stood up and stared at her. Standing her ground, the biologist refused to abandon the wolf.

The noise of the approaching jeep broke the silence and caused the bear to back off a few yards. Using the opportunity, Boyd moved closer to her wolf. The bear's hesitation lasted only a few moments—it again came toward the wolf. When it got to within a few yards, Aluzas sounded the jeep's horn. Confused by the new sound, the bear retreated again.

Boyd ran to the wolf and picked her up. The animal now was regaining consciousness and might bite in self-defense. Holding the wolf's head away from her body, she began walking the seventy-five yards to the jeep. Aluzas jumped out of the idling vehicle, rushed over, and helped her carry the awakening wolf.

They managed to reach the jeep before the bear regained its confidence. Throwing the wolf in first, then climbing in them-selves, the two biologists drove to a safe location, put the wolf out on the ground, and waited for her to recover fully. That wolf, called 8756, later became the alpha female of the South Camas pack. In 1990, Boyd captured and placed a radio collar on one of her daughters. That female was the fourth generation of the Wolf Ecology Project's radio-collared wolves.

Knowing the local wolves as well as she does, Boyd must find it hard to deal with the legal and illegal killing of many of the animals. Nineteen of the thirty-nine wolves she has radio collared have been shot, trapped, or poisoned. Many uncollared wolves also have died. Without the presence of the project's researchers and volunteers in the area, the number of wolves illegally killed no doubt would be much higher.

The documentation and study of the historic reestablishment of wolves in Glacier National Park is now at a critical crossroads. Budget cutbacks have severely hindered the work of the Wolf Ecology Project; private funding will have to supply more support if work is to continue.

In 1987, as wolves were recolonizing Glacier National Park, a report entitled *The Northern Rocky Mountain Wolf Recovery Plan* was approved and published. This document was a joint effort of the U.S. Fish and Wildlife Service (USFWS) and the Northern Rocky Mountain Wolf Recovery Team, a committee of representatives of federal and state agencies, university researchers, conservation organizations, Native tribes, and livestock interests. The USFWS is the federal agency assigned the primary responsibility

(continued on page 106)

The Red Wolf:
A Return to Great Smoky Mountains National Park

The red wolf once was the dominant predator in the southeast region of North America. This wolf, known to science as *Canis rufus*, is smaller and lankier than its close relative, the gray wolf (*Canis lupus*).

According to Ron Nowak, a taxonomist with the U.S. Fish and Wildlife Service (USFWS), all modern wolf species are likely descended from the red wolf. Based on his study of wolf skeletons, both modern and fossilized, Nowak believes that the red wolf originated in North America about one million years ago. During one of the Ice Ages, some red wolves migrated to Asia via the Bering Land Bridge. The gray wolf evolved from that stock about 300,000 years ago and later invaded North America. This species eventually took over the continent, evicting its smaller cousin, the red wolf, from all of its former domain except for what is now the southeastern states. As Nowak colorfully puts it, "The situation was like a tough, overgrown son returning to muscle in on his aging, bantam father."

By the 1970s, due to human persecution and habitat loss, the red wolf was nearly extinct in the wild. The last survivors lived in southwest Louisiana and southeast Texas. The population was so low that many individuals, unable to find mates, bred with coyotes. The resulting hybrids further threatened the viability of red wolves as a species.

Knowing the species was nearly extinct, the USFWS fashioned a recovery plan. Biologist Curtis Carley was assigned the task of determining the species' status and saving it from extinction. He put together a team that caught the last known wild red wolves. Only forty-three of the more than four hundred captured animals appeared to be full-blooded red wolves. Those animals were sent to a breeding facility at Point Defiance Zoo in Tacoma, Washington.

Breeding experiments then were conducted to test the offspring of the captives for evidence of coyote hybridization. Any animal that produced suspect pups was removed from the program. Eventually just seventeen individuals could be certified as pure red wolves. That precariously low number represented the total known population of the species. Fourteen of those animals successfully bred and, from that small pool, the captive red wolf population grew steadily. Soon the Port Defiance Zoo shipped extra wolves to other breeding facilities across the country.

Once the species was reproducing in captivity, the USFWS began to plan a reintroduction program. Experimental releases took place on islands off the Atlantic Coast to develop reintroduction techniques. Meanwhile, biologists searched the south for a suitable release site. In 1984, as the search continued, the Prudential Life Insurance Company generously donated a 118,000-acre tract of land along the northeast coast of North Carolina to the U.S. Government. The donated land became the Alligator River National Wildlife Refuge, the site for the first red wolf reintroduction.

In the fall of 1987, biologists released four pairs of red wolves into the refuge. In subsequent years, the USFWS turned loose additional wolves. Most of the former captives adjusted well to freedom. Any wolves that left the refuge were captured and rereleased or returned to the captive breeding program. During the first five years of the project, at least twenty-three pups were born in the wild, a sure sign of the program's viability. As of early 1993, thirty free-ranging wolves inhabited the refuge. For the first time in history, a species extinct in the wild had been successfully restored to part of its original range.

The progress at Alligator River led to consideration of a second reintroduction site. The USFWS in cooperation with the National Park Service evaluated the 500,000-acre Great Smoky Mountains National Park, located along the mountainous border of Tennessee and North Carolina, as the next possible area. In November of 1991, biologists released a pair of red wolves and two of their captive-born pups into the Cade's Cove section of the park. This was considered an experimental release, a pilot project to determine the feasibility of a larger-scale reintroduction plan.

The initial phase of the project ended in the fall of 1992 when those wolves were recaptured. After evaluating the experiment, the Park Service and USFWS approved a full-fledged reintroduction plan for the Smokies. In October 1992, a pair of wolves and four of their pups were turned loose in Cade's Cove. Two months later, biologists released another family of six at a backcountry site.

Now that these twelve wolves are in the park, the goal of the Smoky Mountain reintroduction project—a self-sustaining population of fifty to seventy-five red wolves in the park and surrounding federal lands—appears to be achievable. Success with this first wolf reintroduction into a national park will facilitate approval of similar projects in other parks and wilderness areas.

Above: An adult red wolf, photographed at Great Smoky Mountains National Park, shortly before the first experimental reintroduction of wolves into the park. Right: A red wolf pup in Great Smoky Mountains National Park. In the spring of 1993, both pairs of reintroduced adult red wolves denned and successfully produced pups. Including those pups, the total population of captive and free-ranging red wolves now numbers approximately 250. (Photos courtesy of Great Smoky Mountains National Park)

Bringing the Wolf Back to Colorado

The last wolf in Colorado was killed in 1945 by a government hunter in the South San Juan Mountains, a range in the southwestern section of the state.

In 1991, forty-six years later, three Colorado residents formed an organization named Sinapu, the Ute word for "wolves." The small group designed an extremely effective program to educate people about wolves and to promote the idea of returning the wolf to Colorado. With the urging of Sinapu, David Skaggs, a Colorado congressman, won approval for a $50,000 feasibility study on restoring wolves to the state. That study began in the spring of 1993 and is expected to be completed in twelve to eighteen months.

If the study determines that one or more sections of Colorado public lands would be suitable for wolf reintroduction programs, the U.S. Fish and Wildlife Service may then list Colorado as a designated recovery area in *The Northern Rocky Mountain Wolf Recovery Plan*. By then, wolf reintroduction could already be underway in Yellowstone. If that project succeeds, Colorado could be the next Rocky Mountain state to experience a return of the wolf.

All this was set in motion by just three people dedicated to wolf issues. Sinapu's success proves that just a handful of people can accomplish great things for wolves. For more information about Sinapu, see page 119.

Alaska's Proposed Aerial Wolf Control Program

Alaska is home to six to seven thousand wolves, about 78 percent of all the wild gray wolves in the United States. The state's wolf density is approximately one wolf per eighty square miles.

In November of 1992, in a move that shocked many, the Alaska Board of Game approved a five-year aerial control project that would kill up to 80 percent of the wolves in three management zones northeast of Anchorage. David Kellyhouse, director of the Alaska Division of Wildlife Conservation (a section of the Alaska Department of Fish and Game), explained the purpose of the wolf control program to *The New York Times:* "We feel we are going to create a wildlife spectacle on a par with the major migrations in East Africa. Mom and pop from Syracuse can come up here and see something that they can't see anywhere else on earth." The real reason for the wolf control plan was clearly stated by Ken Pitcher, the south-central supervisor for the Alaska Department of Fish and Game. Pitcher told *The Boston Globe,* "We're trying to manipulate the system to produce more animals for hunters."

Alaska's proposed wolf control plan received intensive media coverage on network news shows and in newspapers and magazines. Those stories set off howls of protest across the country. According to *The New York Times*, tens of thousands of letters, faxes, and phone calls inundated Alaska, protesting the plan. Many of the messages came from people that might be called "mom and pop from Syracuse," ordinary folks who had been planning a trip to Alaska to see the wildlife.

Alaska magazine printed several typical letters on the wolf control project. One man from California wrote "My wife and I have long planned on a dream vacation to Denali, but if the wolf hunt goes on we plan to boycott Alaska." Another California reader said "If you enact this plan, I will personally forestall a planned summer vacation to Alaska, and I will direct my firm to no longer purchase any products obtained from Alaska." A Washington state woman wrote "Alaska obviously does not value its wildlife. I am sickened at the wolves and the other wildlife being slaughtered. The wildlife, of course, was the reason for our planned Alaskan trips. As I am canceling the plans, I no longer need *Alaska* magazine."

National conservation and environmental organizations, especially The Fund for Animals, called for a international tourists' boycott of Alaska. The Alaska Tourism Marketing Council commissioned a survey of tourists who had previously expressed interest in visiting Alaska and found that the boycott could cost the state at least $86 million in 1993 if the aerial wolf control program went into effect. In the face of that threat, Governor Hickel, owner of the largest hotel in downtown Anchorage, canceled the plan. The Alaska Game Board will reconsider modified versions of the plan (such as allowing the public to hunt wolves with the "land and shoot" method), but for now, thanks to the thousands of people who spoke up for the wolf, the original project is scuttled.

The Alaska controversy and the public's reaction to it shows how far we have come on wolf-related issues. Not so many decades ago, wolf extermination was the official policy of the federal government. Very few people ever questioned the wisdom of the policy or the methods used to carry out that policy. This recent announcement of a wolf control program in Alaska outraged a large portion of the American public.

People from all parts of the county, from all economic backgrounds, from all walks of life, sent a potent message to the Alaska Game Board: We value wolves and demand that they not be killed to satisfy the desires of special interest groups. The leaders of the Alaskan tourism industry quickly discovered that tourists considered the opportunity to see wild wolves a major attraction, a prime reason to visit Alaska. Wolves, once exterminated for economic reasons, may now be protected for the economic benefits they generate.

Left: *An anonymous ad in the* Fairbanks News-Miner *newspaper that satirized the proposed tourists' boycott of Alaska. Despite the perception that Alaskans strongly backed the aerial wolf control proposal, a majority of residents actually opposed the plan. The Alaska-based Dittman Research Corporation asked a cross-section of Alaskans the following question: "Do you support or oppose state agency personnel shooting wolves from helicopters and airplanes?" In response, 74 percent stated they opposed the plan, while only 19 percent supported it. Below: Photographers and wolf in Denali National Park. The high value that tourists now place on seeing a wolf in the wild became a compelling economic reason for the state of Alaska to cancel a proposed aerial wolf control program.*

of enforcing the Endangered Species Act and coordinating the return of the wolf to its former range. Ironically, back in 1915, when the USFWS was called the U.S. Bureau of Biological Survey, Congress ordered the agency to direct the federal wolf extermination program.

The plan outlined steps for wolf recovery in the region and set as a primary goal the establishment at least ten breeding pairs of wolves in three key former ranges: northwest Montana, central Idaho, and the greater Yellowstone area, the ecosystem that includes the national park, and nearby national forests and wilderness areas. On their own, wolves are recolonizing Montana and Idaho. The return of the wolf to Yellowstone, due to its geographic isolation from existing wolf populations, may require what would amount to an affirmative action program.

WOLVES FOR YELLOWSTONE

For millions of years, wolves and their ancestors roamed the area we now call Yellowstone National Park. The wolf became the dominant predator of such wildlife as elk, deer, bison, and moose. To cope with the presence of wolves, those prey species evolved ways of escaping predation. Some acquired the speed to outrun wolves, others grew big enough to fight off a pack, and all developed the alertness to sense danger. More than any other factor, the wolf shaped those species into their modern form.

The traits we so admire in deer and elk and other wild game—speed, grace, agility, and alertness—are conspicuously absent in domestic animals like cows and sheep. Thousands of years of domestication and protection have devolved those species into soulless caricatures of their wild ancestors. If the wolf and their prey are allowed to compete, we will end up with species like deer and elk. Spiritless animals who have the disposition of cows and sheep are the end-product of wolf-free ecosystems.

To survive as a species, the wolves also had to evolve and adapt. Improvements in speed, intelligence, and group-hunting techniques served as counteradaptations to the advantages possessed by their target prey. With these skills and traits, the wolves could catch the more vulnerable members of the wildlife community. So it went in Yellowstone for unknown millennia. Wolves and their prey both thrived in this arena of coevolution.

A few decades after the area became a national park, the managers of Yellowstone exterminated the wolf, one of the ecosystem's major players. According to current National Park Service (NPS) policy, the primary function of Yellowstone is to preserve the area's original ecosystem and the dynamic, natural processes that perpetuate that system. Yellowstone, without a wolf population, fails to truthfully represent that natural state. Like a complicated machine with a vital component missing, the Yellowstone ecosystem will never function properly until that missing element, the wolf, is restored to its rightful place. Robert Barbee, the current superintendent of Yellowstone, made this point in a 1986 statement: "We all here in Yellowstone believe that biologically the case is clear—the wolf is an important missing link and it should be here."

The NPS has understood this truth for some time. Going back at least as far as the 1960s, Yellowstone rangers and biologists have spoken out for the need to reestablish wolves in the park. The importance of wolf restoration in Yellowstone escalated when wolves became a protected endangered species in 1973. The 1987 *Northern Rocky Mountain Wolf Recovery Plan* proposed releasing wolves back into their original range in Yellowstone. If the reintroduction meets the goal of the Recovery Plan (a minimum wolf population in the Yellowstone area of at least ten reproducing pairs for three consecutive years), wolves would be considered recovered and could be removed from the local endangered species list.

Biologically, there is no question that wolves belong in the Yellowstone ecosystem. Politically, the proposal to restore wolves has set off great controversy. The debate over wolves and Yellowstone has raged for years and will continue to do so for many more.

Of the groups opposed to Yellowstone wolf reintroduction, the livestock industry is the most vocal. To the people in this business, wolves threaten economic hardship and symbolize big government interference in their lives. With the specter of government-released wolves killing cattle and sheep haunting their minds, most Yellowstone area ranchers resist reintroducing wolves into the park.

Some wolves probably will stray beyond the park boundary, and a few of them may kill sheep and cows. To make an intelligent prediction on the possible scale of wolf predation on livestock, it is worth looking at the experience of other areas where wolves and domestic animals live in proximity.

The wolf population in Minnesota is approximately 1,550 to 1,750. In an average year, Minnesota wolves kill cattle, sheep, and turkeys on about one out of every three hundred farms located in wolf range. The level of predation amounts to around one-hundredth of 1 percent of the local cattle and one-fourth of 1 percent

Hellroaring Creek, Yellowstone National Park. Since this section of the park once was home to the original wolf population, the area would be an ideal location for reintroducing wolves back into Yellowstone.

of nearby sheep. Although these wolf predation rates are extremely low, the state of Minnesota has set up a compensation and control program to aid any land owner who experiences problems with wolves: Livestock owners receive reimbursements for documented losses to wolves and depredating wolves are captured and relocated or killed by federal agents.

In British Columbia, the province's 6,300 wolves kill about one-fiftieth of 1 percent of neighboring cattle and one-twentieth of 1 percent of local sheep each year. The recovering Montana wolves' rate of predation on livestock is well below the previous figures. They kill an average of just three cows and two sheep annually, a rate that translates to roughly one out of every 25,000 cows (1/250th of 1 percent) and one out of every 5,500 sheep (1/50 of 1 percent) available to them.

Biologist Steve Fritts helped investigate and compile the surprisingly low rates of wolf predation on livestock in Minnesota and Montana. Steve theorizes that wolves are programmed with a search image for the wild natural prey of their area. Since cows and sheep don't match that search image, most wolves pass them by and continue to seek out other targets that do fit their mental image of what prey should look like: deer, elk, moose, beaver, rabbits, hares, and squirrels.

To put these wolf predation numbers in perspective, look at the number of domestic sheep killed by loose dogs in Montana. According to the Montana Agricultural Statistics Service, state ranchers reported a total of 3,500 sheep killed by loose dogs in 1991. As just mentioned, wolves kill an average of just two sheep per year in Montana. Based on those figures, sheep in Montana are 1,750 times more likely to be killed by a dog than by a wolf.

Some people oppose wolf reintroductions because they fear wolves would kill pet dogs. Approximately 34,000 dogs live in the portions of Minnesota that have wolf populations. In recent years, just three dogs per year (about one in 11,000) have been taken by wolves. Any Minnesotan wolf proven to be a dog killer is captured and relocated or destroyed. During my fifteen years in Alaska, our local community had two to three hundred pet dogs and sled dogs. These dogs lived in and often traveled through wolf territories, but as far as I know, none was ever killed by a wolf.

Experts expect the Yellowstone wolf population to eventually stabilize, perhaps twenty years after the initial reintroduction, at a level of about 150 animals, far lower than the Minnesota or British Columbia wolf densities. The numbers of cattle and sheep that graze near the Yellowstone boundary are only a small fraction of the livestock that live near wolves in the other areas. Because grazing on Yellowstone area public land takes place mainly in the summer, the period of livestock exposure to wolves would be much shorter than in Minnesota, where many animals are left outside all year.

Lack of natural wild prey would not be a problem for Yellowstone wolves. Wolf expert L. David Mech described Yellowstone by saying, "I've never seen an area with a denser prey base." Based on current wildlife population numbers, Mech estimates there will be as many as three hundred big game animals for every wolf. That ratio of prey per wolf is among the highest known to wolf researchers.

In 1985, NPS director William Penn Mott told conservation groups that creation of a private fund to reimburse ranchers for wolf-killed livestock could alleviate much of the opposition to wolf reintroduction in Yellowstone. Defenders of Wildlife, in particular their northern Rockies regional representative, Hank Fischer, turned that suggestion into reality in 1987. Defenders explained the need for such a fund to the conservation community and raised over $100,000.

If a wolf does kill a rancher's animal, the Defenders' Wolf Restoration Fund covers the financial loss. Hank Fischer explained his organization's program by stating: "Our goal has been to shift any economic burden associated with wolf recovery away from the individual livestock producer and onto the willing shoulders of the millions of wolf supporters around the country."

In 1992, Defenders established a wolf reward program that awards a landowner $5,000 if a litter of wolf pups is successfully reared on his or her property. This "free-market environmentalism" enables pro-wolf individuals to pay property owners to supply wolf habitat. The brilliance of this program is that it transforms wolves into financial assets rather than liabilities for landowners. These innovative programs developed by Defenders of Wildlife demonstrate that conservation groups can provide effective, workable solutions to complex issues.

Before any wolves are released into Yellowstone, a well-defined system of dealing with problem wolves will be delineated. A special provision of the Endangered Species Act allows reintroduced animals, such as the wolf, to be classified as "experimental populations." This option, if selected, could provide the necessary flexibility to manage wolves that create conflicts.

Under the experimental population designation, any wolf that leaves the park and preys on livestock will be immediately targeted by federal or state wildlife managers. The offending wolf will be captured and relocated to an area without stock. Under some circumstances, the targeted wolf will be destroyed or kept in permanent captivity.

Capture of any problem Yellowstone wolves could be facilitated by fitting each released animal with a "capture collar"—a collar containing a transmitter, receiver, computer, and tranquilizer dart. A radio signal orders the computer to inject an immobi-

Yellowstone has one of the highest prey densities in the lower forty-eight states, so a reintroduced wolf population would have plenty of game available to them.

lizing drug into the neck of the wolf. This new technology enables biologists to catch specific wolves in record time.

Quick action in dealing with problem wolves will, in the long term, increase public support for reintroduction programs. Problem wolves, if allowed to continue to prey on livestock, would cause embittered members of the public to feel justified in shooting any wolf they see. For the good of the recovering wolf population and the safety of nonoffending wolves, any livestock-killing wolves must be removed promptly. Pro-wolf groups must accept this as part of the cost of returning wolves to Yellowstone.

To summarize the wolf-livestock issue, it first must be emphasized that wolves in other areas kill very few domestic animals. The Yellowstone wolves will live in an area with a very high density of wild prey. Numbers of livestock near the park boundary are low. Since any wolf known to be a livestock killer will be either removed or destroyed, and economic losses suffered by ranchers will be reimbursed, it seems reasonable solutions exist to any problems that reintroduced wolves may cause ranchers.

Public opinion polls have documented substantial support for the Yellowstone reintroduction program. A number of polls conducted in the states surrounding Yellowstone show that substan-tially more people in Montana, Wyoming, and Idaho are for wolf reintroduction than against it. A survey conducted in Yellowstone found 82 percent of visitors felt wolves deserved a place in the park. During the summer of 1992, Defenders of Wildlife gave Yellowstone visitors a chance to vote for or against wolf reintroduction in the park. At the end of the season, the "yes" votes accounted for 97.3 percent of the total ballots cast.

In the fall of 1991, Congress authorized the preparation of an Environmental Impact Statement (EIS) on the reintroduction of the wolf into Yellowstone and central Idaho. Part of the EIS process involves extensive opportunities for the public to comment on the issue and possible actions. Assuming the final document, anticipated in early 1994, recommends reintroduction, wolves could be in Yellowstone by 1995. In the meantime, since wolves are recolonizing Montana, a pair could settle in Yellowstone, as the Magic Pack did in Glacier National Park in 1985.

What would be the significance of returning wolves to Yellowstone? First, it will fulfill the mandate of the Endangered Species Act to restore an endangered species to the range it lost through the adverse action of humankind. Second, wolves will help restore Yellowstone's ecosystem to a condition that more closely

(continued on page 113)

Are Wolves Already Back in Yellowstone?

Two events involving wolves and Yellowstone National Park made national news in 1992. In early August, filmmaker Ray Paunovich shot an eleven-minute sequence of a black, wolf like animal interacting with grizzly bears and a coyote in Hayden Valley.

On September 30, Jerry Kysar, while hunting with friends just outside the southeast border of Yellowstone, shot and killed an animal he thought to be a coyote. On examining the dead canine, he knew that it was far too big to be a coyote. Kysar went to the nearest ranger station and reported the incident. When rangers saw the black, ninety-three-pound adult male animal, it appeared to be a wolf. They packed it out of the backcountry and shipped the remains to the U.S. Fish and Wildlife Forensic Laboratory in Ashland, Oregon. The lab took DNA samples from the carcass and began a lengthy process of analysis, hoping to determine if the animal was a true wolf.

Since those events, the Hayden Valley animal has been seen on several other occasions and could still be in the park. Its ability to survive in Yellowstone and its behavior around bears and coyotes fits the pattern of normal wolf behavior. Wolf experts who viewed the film are unable to definitively classify the animal. Its physique does not quite match the classic form of a true wolf. The chest is broader and the legs seem stubbier than wild wolves I have seen in Alaska and Montana. Those features may indicate the animal is something other than a full-blooded *Canis lupus;* perhaps it is a wolf-dog hybrid that either wandered into the park or was turned loose in the area. A much closer sighting or physical examination will be needed to determine its status.

Wolf biologists and park rangers conducted a thorough search of the region where Kysar shot the other animal. The team found no evidence of wolves in the area. The only canine tracks in the search zone were coyote size.

The initial DNA analysis could not determine if the animal was a wolf or a wolf-dog hybrid. Later, the U.S. Fish and Wildlife Service (USFWS) announced that a more detailed study had found that it was a true wolf and that it was closely related to a female wolf that biologist Diane Boyd had radio collared in Glacier Na-

tional Park in 1989. This information strongly implies that the Yellowstone wolf had been born in Montana and dispersed south to the park area.

In all the excitement surrounding these events, an important point was often overlooked. The recovery goal for Yellowstone, according to the 1987 *Northern Rocky Mountain Wolf Recovery Plan,* is the establishment of at least ten breeding pairs in the park area. Sightings of occasional wolflike animals have occurred before in Yellowstone, but to date wolves have not produced a viable, self-sustaining population. No matter how you add it up, one dead wolf, and one possible live wolf, does not make a recovered population.

The USFWS biologists that now are writing the Environmental Impact Statement (EIS) on Yellowstone wolf recovery are studying all possible options that might achieve the recovery goal. When they release the EIS, it could recommend that the wolf reintroduction option be postponed so that natural recolonization could occur. If it is proven that wild wolves are dispersing into the park, establishing packs, and producing pups, the natural recovery process could continue at its own pace. It might easily take many decades for recolonization to reach the recovery goal of ten breeding pairs. During that time, a poisoning incident, like the one that killed most of the Headwaters Pack near Glacier, could cripple and greatly delay the process. The EIS could also recommend that an experimental reintroduction program be scheduled for Yellowstone. If documented sightings of dispersing wolves later occur in the park, the reintroduction would be regarded as an augmentation to natural recovery. This option would achieve the recovery goal on a far faster timetable than recolonization.

The key point to remember in these recent developments is that there is still no evidence of a existing, breeding wolf population in Yellowstone. Defenders of Wildlife, in the December 1992 issue of their *Wolf Action* newsletter, places the controversy in its proper perspective: "Our position on [natural] recovery vs. reintroduction for Yellowstone is simple: reintroduce unless there's hard evidence of an existing population."

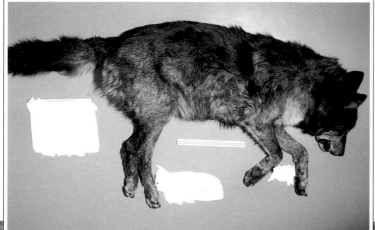

Left: A U.S. Fish and Wildlife Service photo of the wolf that was shot and killed just outside of Yellowstone in the fall of 1992. (Photo courtesy of the National Fish and Wildlife Forensic Laboratory, U.S. Fish and Wildlife Service, Ashland, Oregon.)

Above: Wolf 8962, born in Glacier National Park in 1988. Genetic samples from this wolf taken by Diane Boyd closely matched DNA material from the wolf killed outside Yellowstone in 1992, proving that the two animals were related. (Photo by Diane Boyd.)
Right: A frame from the 16mm film of the black, wolflike animal seen in the Hayden Valley of Yellowstone in August of 1992. It is passing a family of grizzly bears who had just fed on a bison carcass. (Photo courtesy of Busch Productions.)

Above: *Based on experience elsewhere, wolf predation rates on livestock outside Yellowstone should be extremely minimal.* Facing page: *Restoring wolves to Yellowstone National Park will return the ecosystem to its original balance.*

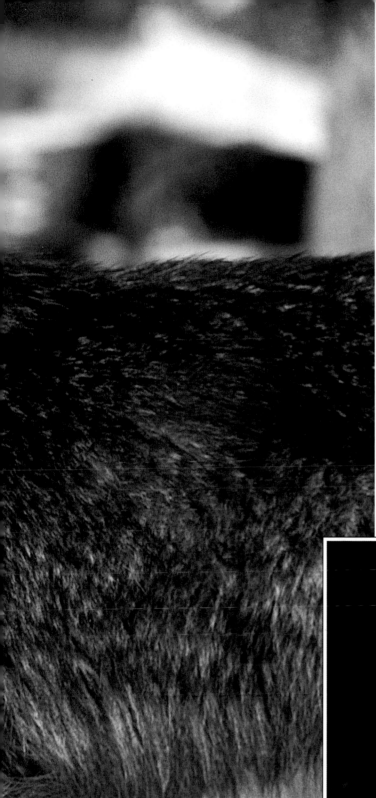

resembles the way the system originally functioned. A critically important missing component, a large predator, will be reinstated to its rightful place in Yellowstone. With wolves again roaming the park, visitors to Yellowstone will experience a natural, complex ecosystem that is essentially complete. The idea of the national park—now evolved to mean conservation of the integrity of the original ecosystem—will be closer to reality.

Once wolves return to Yellowstone, natural interactions between predators and prey also will be restored. The wolves, as Adolph Murie found in Alaska, will selectively target the weakest and most vulnerable members of the populations of deer, elk, bison, and other wildlife. Such a selection process will enhance the health and vigor of the park's game species.

The successful return of wolves to Yellowstone will be symbolic of a new attitude toward wolf society by human society. It was our species that exterminated the wolf in Yellowstone and from 99 percent of its original range in the lower forty-eight states. Now, many in our society have come to understand the value of allowing nature to work out its own balance in at least a few protected areas. Yellowstone, the first and most famous national park, with wolves again roaming within its boundaries, will be the proof that our species has finally learned to share the earth with a kindred species.

In August 1992, the U.S. Fish and Wildlife Service held a hearing in Helena, Montana, on the issue of reintroducing wolves into Yellowstone. During the hearing, Jack Gladstone, a spokesman for the Blackfeet Tribal Council, read a resolution supporting the concept of returning wolves to the park. In explaining his tribe's attitude toward wolves, Jack made the following statement: "We looked upon animals like the wolf, buffalo, elk, and grizzly bear as elders because they were already established here in the creation when our people came along. Ours is the task to respect the elders and to respect what the elders teach us."

EPILOGUE: THE SPIRIT OF A WOLF

A FEW THOUSAND WORDS AND A FEW DOZEN PHOTOGRAPHS seem so inadequate to convey the spirit of the wolf. There is far more to the wolf than any human can comprehend. Despite all the similarities in social behavior between us and wolves, they are still a mystery. Perhaps that is why wolves have always fascinated our race.

After finishing this book, I felt that there was something I needed to do. Because the tragic story of Rags the Digger wouldn't leave my mind, I made a pilgrimage to his old home range in western Colorado. I spent two days in his former territory, trying to understand the meaning of his life and what that life might symbolize. The land, several thousand square miles just south of Dinosaur National Monument, once had been prime wolf habitat, but no wolves had lived here since the 1920s, the time of Rags's death.

Something important was missing in this country, an element whose absence made the land seem empty and impoverished. That missing component was the spirit of the wolf. As I thought of these things I remembered a passage written by Henry David Thoreau that voiced the feelings I had. Because I grew up in Massachusetts, a few miles from Thoreau's cabin at Walden Pond, and often walked through the woods that inspired his writings, his words hold special meaning for me. On March 23, 1856, after one of his daily treks in the forests of Massachusetts, Thoreau wrote:

> But when I consider that the nobler animals have been exterminated here—the cougar, panther, lynx, wolverine, wolf, bear, moose, deer, the beaver, the turkey, etc.—I cannot but feel as if I lived in a tamed, and, as it were, emasculated country . . . I seek acquaintance with Nature—to know her moods and manners. Primitive Nature is the most interesting to me. I take infinite pains to know all the phenomena of the spring, for instance, thinking that I have here the entire poem, and then, to my chagrin, I hear that it is but an imperfect copy that I possess and have read, that my ancestors have torn out many of the first leaves and grandest passages, and mutilated it in many places. I should not like to think that some demigod had come before me and picked out some of the best of the stars. I wish to know an entire heaven and an entire earth.

Without Rags and his kin, this was an emasculated land, a place that might be safe for cows and sheep, but a country that had lost its spirit.

One evening, I found a spot that overlooked the Rio Blanco, a river that seventy years ago Rags must have used for drinking water. As I walked the ground, the site seemed heavy with his presence. Then an idea for a ceremony came to me. I returned to my car, grabbed a tape player and a cassette tape and climbed up to a high point that I thought Rags would have liked. Among a scattering of juniper trees and sage brush, I played a song called *Wolf*, written and sung by a friend named Jack Gladstone, a Blackfeet Indian. Like his ancestors, Jack has deep feelings for wolves, and his song skillfully conveys the attitude of respect that Native Americans have toward the wolf and their sadness at its departure from its homeland. Playing the song seemed the ideal way to honor the spirit of Rags. With Jack's permission, I'll print three stanzas of his song:

> Wolf, you were free, you were hunting in the sun.
> Long before man arrived, you were nature, you were young.
> Then we came and survived, we were brothers side by side
> In the days of the arrow, in the days of the bow.
> In the days of the spirit, not too long a time ago.

> Wolf, you were seen, by the fathers of our dream
> And the hunt you engaged was the blueprint for our age.
> Then we learned and we burned with desire to know more
> In the dawn that was man's, they hunted o'er the plains.
> Still the wolf pack set the pace, when the fire was just a flame.

> Wolf, where are you in the lower forty-eight?
> Once you ran through the woods of the eastern seaboard states!
> Now you're gone from the woods, from the mountains, from the plains;
> They are filled with the still of a vanishing frontier,
> They are broken by the blade, tilling all we once held dear.

In the middle of Jack's song, a thunderstorm swept in and pounded the earth with lightning bolts and heavy rain. As the music faded out, I felt I had to add some of my own words to complete the tribute to Rags. Looking over his old home range, standing in the downpour, I silently apologized for what had been done to him and his family. I prayed that someday his spirit might live again in the body of another wolf.

Walking back to my car, I experienced a flash of revelation. Rags's spirit, almost certainly, had already been reborn. Native Americans say that the spirit of an animal, especially one as tough as Rags, never dies but lives on in a succession of new bodies. I

know two wolves who may have been born with Rags's indomitable spirit.

The limping male of the East Fork Pack equaled Rags in courage and tenacity. As a young wolf, he got caught in a steel leg trap but yanked his foot free. The injured paw never healed, and he had to face life with a severe handicap. Overcoming tremendous adversity, he not only survived but became the alpha male of his pack, fathered and raised many litters of pups. In old age, he challenged a five-hundred-pound moose to a fight to the death. Like Rags, he died a good death.

If a living wolf has Rags's spirit, it must be the alpha female of the Headwaters Pack, who lives next to Glacier National Park. When her mate and fellow wolves were poisoned, she suddenly became the pack's only survivor. Pregnant and without help, she

The original home range of Rags the Digger, Rio Blanco County, Colorado.

dug out a den and awaited the arrival of her pups. After their birth, despite her weakened condition, she managed to hunt and provide for them. That two of her pups reached adulthood is an accomplishment of heroic dimensions.

As I was about to write this section, I spoke with Diane Boyd about recent developments in the Headwaters Pack. She had just flown over the pack's territory and saw the alpha female with a new mate and two other adult wolves that must have been her pups from the previous year. Scattered among the adults were seven new pups! This wolf's fierce determination to triumph over the devastating poisoning episode demonstrates the same type of unimaginable courage that enabled Rags to endure when his family was also wiped out.

Rags the Digger, the limping East Fork male, the Headwaters Pack alpha female—these individuals all symbolize the power and character of the wolf spirit and its ability to prevail over the worst adversity. It is a spirit that our race once vowed to destroy. Fortunately, despite the full force of the federal government and the use of thousands of tons of poison, that spirit proved too strong for us to extinguish.

Now we have the opportunity to rectify our past mistreatment of wolves. I think Thoreau hit upon the ultimate reason to restore wolves to their rightful place in creation. Without wolves, we do live in an emasculated land. The only way we can truly experience "an entire heaven and an entire earth" is to bring the wolf back. If we can accomplish that, perhaps we may earn the honor of being called a kindred species by the wolf.

How to Become Involved with Wolf Issues

NONPROFIT ORGANIZATIONS INVOLVED WITH WOLF ISSUES

ALASKA WILDLIFE ALLIANCE
Box 202022
Anchorage, Alaska 99520

DEFENDERS OF WILDLIFE
1244 19th Street NW
Washington, DC 20036

INTERNATIONAL WOLF CENTER
1396 Highway 169
Ely, Minnesota 55731

ISLE ROYALE WOLF-MOOSE STUDY
Michigan Tech Fund/Alumni House
Michigan Technological University
Houghton, Michigan 49931

MEXICAN WOLF COALITION OF NEW MEXICO
7239 Isleta Boulevard SW
Albuquerque, New Mexico 87105

MEXICAN WOLF COALITION OF TEXAS
Box 1526
Spring, Texas 77383

MISSION: WOLF
Box 211
Silver Cliff, CO 81249

NATIONAL WILDLIFE FEDERATION
1400 Sixteenth Street NW
Washington, DC 20036

PRESERVE ARIZONA'S WOLVES
1413 East Dobbins Road
Phoenix, Arizona 85040

RED WOLF RECOVERY FUND
National Fish and Wildlife Foundation
18th and C Streets NW
Washington, DC 20240

THE RED WOLF FUND
Tacoma Zoological Society
5400 North Pearl Street
Tacoma, Washington 98407

SINAPU
Box 3243
Boulder, Colorado 80307

WOLF ECOLOGY PROJECT
School of Forestry
University of Montana
Missoula, Montana 59812

WOLF EDUCATION FUND
Zion Natural History Association
Springdale, Utah 84767

THE WOLF FUND
Box 471
Moose, Wyoming 83012

WOLF HAVEN
3111 Offut Lake Road
Tenino, Washington 98589

Newsletters and Magazines on Wolf Issues

The addresses for these organizations are listed in "Nonprofit Organizations Involved with Wolf Issues," or with the name of the publication.

Wolf Action, published by Defenders of Wildlife, is available free of charge.

International Wolf magazine is sent by the International Wolf Center to its membership.

The Red Wolf Newsletter is produced by the Tacoma Zoological Society.

Lobo Howl: The Mexican Wolf Recovery Newsletter, a publication that deals with wolf issues in the Southwest, can be acquired from the Mexican Wolf Coalition of Texas.

Colorado Wolf Tracks, published by Sinapu (the Ute word for "wolf"), covers wolf issues in Colorado.

Paw Prints, a quarterly newsletter on wolf issues in Arizona, is published by Preserve Arizona's Wolves.

The Spirit, the newsletter of the Alaska Wildlife Alliance, reports on wolf issues in the state of Alaska.

Wolf! magazine can be ordered by writing to: Wolf!, Box 29, Lafayette, Indiana 47902.

Wolves in the Northern Rockies: Commonly Asked Questions, a publication of the Northern Rockies Natural Resource Center, 240 North Higgins, Missoula, Montana 59802.

Making Your Voice Heard

We are all joint owners of America's national parks, national forests, and other public lands. It is your right and responsibility to voice your opinion on how those lands should be managed. Now is the time to get involved with the issue of wolf reintroduction in Yellowstone and in the Southwest. Environmental Impact Statements (EIS) are now being prepared by the U.S. Fish and Wildlife Service on both issues. To get on their mailing list or to comment on those possible reintroductions, write:

Yellowstone Wolf EIS
Box 8017
Helena, Montana 59601

Mexican Wolf EIS
Box 1306
Albuquerque, New Mexico 87103

An East Fork wolf rests after chasing, but failing to catch, a caribou.

Mother wolf about to gently pick up a wayward five-week-old pup and carry it back to the den.

References and Suggested Readings on Wolves

Allen, Durward L. 1979. *The Wolves of Minong: Their Vital Role in a Wild Community*. Boston: Houghton Mifflin Company.

Bass, Rick. 1992. *The Ninemile Wolves*. Livingston, Montana: Clark City Press.

Bowden, Charles. 1992. Lonesome Lobo. *Wildlife Conservation*. January/February, 1992.

Brown, David, editor. 1983. *The Wolf in the Southwest*. Tucson: University of Arizona Press.

Brown, William. 1991. *A History of the Denali-Mount McKinley Region, Alaska*. Santa Fe, New Mexico: National Park Service Southwest Regional Office.

Burbank, James. 1990. *Vanishing Lobo*. Boulder, Colorado: Johnson Books.

Cahalane, Victor. 1939. The Evolution of Predator Control Policy in the National Parks. *Journal of Wildlife Management*. 3(3):229-237.

Cameron, Jenks. 1929. *The Bureau of Biological Survey: Its History, Activities, and Organization*. Baltimore: The Johns Hopkins Press.

Carhart, Arthur, and Stanley Young. 1929. *The Last Stand of the Pack*. New York: J.H. Sears and Company.

Crisler, Lois. 1958. *Arctic Wild*. New York: Harper and Brothers.

Curnow, Edward. 1969. *The History of the Eradication of the Wolf in Montana*. Master's Thesis. Missoula: University of Montana.

Day, Albert, and Almer Nelson. 1928. *Wild Life Conservation and Control in Wyoming Under the Leadership of the United States Biological Survey*. Laramie: The University of Wyoming.

Emerson, Everett. 1976. *Letters From New England: The Massachusetts Bay Colony 1629-1638*. Amherst: The University of Massachusetts Press.

Flader, Susan. 1974. *Thinking Like a Mountain: Aldo Leopold and the Evolution of an Ecological Attitude Toward Deer, Wolves, and Forests*. Columbia: University of Missouri Press.

Hall, Roberta, and Henry Sharp, editors. 1978. *Wolf and Man—Evolution in Parallel*. New York: Academic Press.

Harding, A.W. 1960. The Wolf in Scotland. *The Scots Magazine*. December 1960.

Harrington, Fred, and Paul Paquet, editors. 1982. *Wolves of the World*. Pine Ridge, New Jersey: Noyes Publications.

International Wolf Center. 1992. *Wolves of the High Arctic*. Stillwater, Minnesota: Voyageur Press, Inc.

Leopold, Aldo. 1949. *A Sand County Almanac*. New York: Oxford University Press.

Lopez, Barry Holstun. 1978. *Of Wolves and Men*. New York: Charles Scribner's Sons.

Matthiessen, Peter. 1959. *Wildlife in America*. New York: Viking.

McClintock, Walter. [1910] 1968. *The Old North Trail*. Reprint. Lincoln: University of Nebraska Press.

Mech, L. David. [1970] 1981. *The Wolf: The Ecology and Behavior of an Endangered Species*. Reprint. Minneapolis: University of Minnesota Press.

Mech, L. David. 1988. *The Arctic Wolf: Living with the Pack*. Stillwater, Minnesota: Voyageur Press.

Mech, L. David. 1991. *The Way of the Wolf*. Stillwater, Minnesota: Voyageur Press.

Murie, Adolph. [1944] 1985. *The Wolves of Mount McKinley*. Reprint. Seattle: University of Washington Press.

Nash, Roderick. 1967. *Wilderness and the American Mind*. New Haven, Connecticut: Yale University Press.

Nowak, Ron. 1992. Wolves: The Great Travelers of Evolution. *International Wolf*. Winter 1992.

Rutter, Russell, and Douglas Pimlott. 1968. *The World of the Wolf*. Philadelphia: J.B. Lippincott and Co.

Savage, Candace. 1988. *Wolves*. San Francisco: Sierra Club Books.

Schultz, James Willard. 1901. The Eagle Creek Wolfers. *Forest and Stream*. January 5, 12, and 19, 1901.

Schultz, James Willard. 1916. *Blackfeet Tales of Glacier Park*. Boston: Houghton Mifflin Company.

Schultz, James Willard. 1962. *Blackfeet and Buffalo*. Norman: University of Oklahoma Press.

Schultz, James Willard. 1974. *Why Gone Those Times: Blackfeet Tales by James Willard Schultz*. Norman: The University of Oklahoma Press.

Singer, Francis. 1975. *The History and Status of Wolves in Northern Glacier National Park, Montana*. West Glacier, Montana: Glacier National Park Scientific Paper # 1.

Skinner, Milton. 1927. The Predatory and Fur-Bearing Animals of the Yellowstone National Park. *Roosevelt Wildlife Bulletin*. 4(2):163-282.

Summers, Montague. [1933] 1966. *The Werewolf*. Reprint. New Hyde Park, New York: University Books.

U.S. Fish and Wildlife Service. 1987. *Northern Rocky Mountain Wolf Recovery Plan*. Denver: U.S. Fish and Wildlife Service.

U.S. National Park Service, et al. 1990. *Wolves For Yellowstone? A Report to the U.S. Congress, Volume II*. Yellowstone National Park, Wyoming: National Park Service.

Varley, John, and Wayne Brewster, editors. 1992. *Wolves for Yellowstone? A Report to the U.S. Congress, Volume IV*. Yellowstone National Park, Wyoming: National Park Service.

Vest, Jay. 1988. The Medicine Wolf Returns: Traditional Blackfeet Concepts of *Canis lupus*. *Western Wildlands*. Summer 1988.

Weaver, John. 1978. *The Wolves of Yellowstone*. National Park Service Natural Resources Report #14. Washington: U.S. Government Printing Office.

Young, Stanley. 1942. The War on the Wolf. *American Forest*. November (part one) and December (part two) 1942.

Young, Stanley. 1944. *The Wolves of North America*. (Vol. I) Washington, D.C.: American Wildlife Institute.

Young, Stanley. 1946. *The Wolf in North American History*. Caldwell, Idaho: Caxton Printing.

Index

Adirondack State Forest Preserve, 95
Alaska, 104–105
    wolf population, 98, 104
    wolf control program, 104–105
Allen, Durward, 92–93
Alligator River National Wildlife Refuge, 102
Alpha wolves, 22–23, 30–32, 42–45
    See also Breeding; Social hierarchy
Apache National Forest, 94
Arizona, 75
    reintroduction in, 94–95
Attacks on humans, 18, 24, 27, 40

Baxter State Park, 95
Beta wolves, 33
    See also Alpha wolves; Breeding
Blackfeet and Buffalo, 26
Blackfeet Indians. *See* Native Americans
Bounties on wolves, 24, 36, 40, 65, 67
    in Michigan, 92
    in Minnesota, 79, 92
    in western states, 65, 67
    in Wisconsin, 92
    private, 67
Boyd, Diane, 42, 45, 99–101, 110–111, 117
Breeding, 30–31, 42
    See also Alpha wolves; Inbreeding; Social hierarchy
Breeding programs. *See* Red wolf; Mexican wolf
British Columbia, 95, 98, 108

Canada, 92–93, 98
Canine hepatitus. *See* Diseases
Canine parvovirus. *See* Diseases
Canis lupus. *See* Gray wolf
Canis lupus baileyi. *See also* Mexican wolf
Canis lupus lycaon. *See* Eastern Timber wolf
Canis rufus. *See* Red wolf
Capture collar, 108–109
Caywood, Bill, 70–73
Coevolution, 106
Cole, Martin, 12–13
Control, wolf. *See* Extermination, government programs; National Park Service, predator control policy
Coyote, 41, 57–58, 60–62, 64, 90

hybridization with wolf, 102
Curnow, Edward, 41, 67

Defenders of Wildlife, 108, 110
Defenders Wolf Restoration Fund, 108
Denali National Park and Preserve, 8–10, 12–13
    See also Mount McKinley National Park
Dens, 42–43
Denning. *See* Extermination, methods of
Directions for the Destruction of Wolves and Coyotes, 67
Diseases, 24, 93
    See also Extermination, methods of, contagious diseases
Dog, 108
    hybridization with wolf, 18, 110
Domestic animals. *See* Livestock depredation
Dominance. *See* Social hierarchy

East Fork Pack, 8–16, 46–49, 87–89
Eastern Timber wolf, 39 (range map), 95
Ecology of the Coyote in the Yellowstone, 90
Ecosystem, 93
    See also Yellowstone, ecosystem
Elkins, Steve, 58
Endangered species, 94, 98, 106
Endangered Species Act, 1973, 98, 108–109
    "experimental population" provision, 108
Europe. *See* Old World
Extermination, 24, 65, 67, 75, 82, 84
    as national policy, 10, 90, 104–105
    methods of
        poisoning, 40–41, 51–52, 57, 65, 75, 80
        contagious diseases, 67
        denning, 62, 75, 77
        hunting, 40, 62, 65
        trapping, 62, 65, 70
    government programs, 57–58, 60, 62, 64–65, 67, 75, 90
    See also National Park Service, predator control programs

Food disgorgement. *See* Pups, feeding
Food-begging. *See* Pups, feeding

Fritts, Steve, 30, 80, 108
Fund for Animals, The, 104

Genetic makeup. *See* Breeding; Inbreeding; Reproduction
Glacier National Park, 62–65, 98–101, 106, 110
    recolonization, 98
    reintroduction, 106
    wolf population, 65
Gladstone, Jack, 114, 116
Gray wolf, 10, 67, 77, 92, 104
    range, 38 (map)
    See also Mexican wolf; Eastern Timber wolf; Red wolf
Great Smoky Mountains National Park, 102–103

History of the Eradication of the Wolf in Montana, 67
Howling, 28
Hunting of game species by humans, 51, 104
    compared to hunting by wolves, 28
Hunting by wolves. *See* Pack, hunting
Hunting of wolves. *See* Extermination, methods of, hunting
Hunting associations, 60, 67
Hybridization. *See* Dog, hybridization with wolf; Coyote, hybridization with wolf

Idaho, 99, 106
    reintroduction in, 109
Inbreeding, 45, 93
    See also Breeding
International Wolf Center, 96
Isle Royale National Park, 92–93

Journey to Caribouland, 12

Lacey Act, 57
Langford, Nathaniel, 51
Leopold, Aldo, 91–96
Letters From New England: The Massachusetts Bay Colony 1629–1638, 36

Livestock industry, 60, 67, 106
Livestock depredation, 18, 41, 60, 65, 67, 106, 108–109

rates of, 106, 108
reimbursement programs, 95, 108
Lopez, Barry Holstun, 77, 97–98
Lycopithecus, 18
Lycanthropy. *See* Werewolf
Magic Pack, 98
North Camas Pack, 98, 100
South Camas Pack, 98, 100–101
Spruce Creek Pack, 98
Headwaters Pack, 98–100, 116–117
Maine, 95
Management of wolves in national parks, 12
Mange, 67
Mating. *See* Alpha wolves; Breeding; Inbreeding
Mech, L. David, 13, 92, 96, 108
Mexican wolf, 94–95
range, 38 (map), 94
reintroduction, 39 (map), 94–95,
Mexican Wolf Coalition of Texas, The, 94
Mexican Wolf Compensation Fund, The, 95
Mexico, 77, 94
Michigan, 92
Minnesota, 106, 108
wolf population, 12, 79, 92, 106
Montana, 67, 99, 106, 108
reintroduction in, 109
Mount McKinley National Park, 10–12
wolf control program, 12–13, 90
See also Denali National Park and Preserve
Mount Rainier National Park, 95
Mountain lion, 57–58, 61–62
See also Extermination, government programs; National Park Service, predator control policy
Murie, Adolph, 12–13, 46, 90–91, 113

National Park Service (NPS), 58, 90, 102, 106
Annual Report of the Director, 1918, 58, 65
predator control policy, 58, 60, 65, 90
National Park System, 10
Native Americans, 41, 75, 77, 84, 114
mythology about wolves, 26–27, 36, 116
New Hampshire, 95
New World, 36, 40
New York, 95
Norris, Philetus, 51–52
North Cascades National Park, 95
Northern Rocky Mountain Wolf Recovery Plan, The, 101, 104, 106, 110

Northern Rocky Mountain Wolf Recovery Team, 101

Of Wolves and Men, 77
Old World attitude toward wolves, 18–19, 24
See also Werewolf
Origins of Man, 18

Pack, 20–23, 28, 30
communal care of young, 20, 22, 30, 33
dispersal, 30
hunting, 23 26, 28, 33, 45, 106
See also Pups; Territories of wolves; Social hierarchy
Paquet, Paul, 42
Pelts, wolf, 40–41
Peterson, Rolf, 92–93
Poisoning. *See* Extermination, methods of
Population of wolves, 12, 77
natural controls, 28, 30, 92
See also Breeding; Inbreeding

Preserve Arizona's Wolves, 95
Prey, 13, 64, 92–93
condition of as related to depredation, 28, 30, 90, 92, 106, 109
population density of, 90, 92, 108
search image, 108
Protection, legal. *See* Endangered Species Act, 1973
Pups, 20–23
development, 20, 22–23, 28, 30
feeding, 20, 22
socialization, 20, 22
See also Pack, communal care of young
Rabies, 24
Rags the Digger, 70–73, 115–117
Raised-leg urination, 28
Ranching associations, 67
Range, 38–39 (maps)
carrying capacity of, 30
Read, Carveth, 18
Ream, Robert, 99
Recolonization, 106, 110
Recovery Plan for the Eastern Timber Wolf, 95
Red wolf, 102–103
original range, 38 (map)
reintroduction, 39 (map), 102–103
Reintroduction, 39 (map), 93, 94–95, 102–103, 104, 106, 110
public opinion of, 94–95, 109

Sand County Almanac, A, 96

Scent marking, 28, 30, 42
Search image. *See* Prey, search image
Schultz, James Willard, 26–27, 40, 65, 84
Sinapu, 104
Social hierarchy, 22–23, 28, 33, 30–31, 42, 45
See also Alpha wolves

Territories of wolves, 28, 30, 42
Texas, 94
Thoreau, Henry David, 51, 115
Threatened status. *See* Endangered species
Trapping. *See* Extermination, methods of
U. S. Army in Yellowstone, 52, 55, 57
U. S. Bureau of Biological Survey (USBS), 65, 67, 80
U. S. Fish and Wildlife Service, 65, 94–95, 101, 102, 104, 110
U. S. Forest Service, 67
Washburn-Doane Yellowstone Expedition, 51
Washington state, 95
Washington Department of Wildlife, 95
Weaver, John, 60, 62
Werewolf, 24–25
See also Old World attitude toward wolves
Why Gone Those Times?, 26
Wisconsin, 92
Wolf Ecology Project, *See* University of Montana Wolf Ecology Project
Wolf Haven, 95
Wolf sightings, 95, 110
Wolf (song), 116
"Wolfers," 40, 70
Wolves of Isle Royale, The, 92
Wolves of Minong, The, 92
Wolves of Mount McKinley, The, 13
Wolves of Yellowstone, The, 62

Yellowstone, 50–62, 90, 106–113, 114
ecosystem, 106, 109, 113
Environmental Impact Statement, 109, 110
reintroduction program, 106, 108–109, 110, 114
wildlife prey base, 108
wolf control program, 57–58, 60–62
wolf population, 57, 62, 108
wolf sightings in, 110–111

Acknowledgments

This book was made possible by many people who graciously shared their knowledge of wolves with me. I would like to thank the following individuals:

National Park Service employees: Norm Bishop,* Mark Johnson (DVM),* Wayne Brewster, John Varley, Tom Tankersley,* Lee Whittlesey,* John Mack, and Barbara Zafft (Yellowstone National Park); Cliff Martinka,* Jim Tilmant,* Bruce Fladmark, Cindy Nielsen,* Deirdre Shaw, and Beth Dunagan (Glacier National Park); Joe Van Horn, John Burch, and Tom Meier* (Denali National Park); Bob Miller* (Great Smoky Mountains National Park);

U.S. Fish and Wildlife employees: Steven Fritts* (Northern Rocky Mountain Wolf Coordinator), Ed Bangs* (Team Leader for the Yellowstone Wolf Environmental Impact Statement), Gary Henry* (Red Wolf Coordinator), Mike Phillips* (Alligator River National Wildlife Refuge), Chris Lucash* (red wolf biologist at Great Smoky Mountains National Park), David Parsons* (Mexican Wolf Recovery Coordinator), Steve Fain (U.S. Fish and Wildlife Forensic Laboratory), Sharon Rose, Joy Nicholopoulos,* Doug Zimmer,* L. David Mech,* and Ron Nowak;

Washington Department of Wildlife employees: Scott Fitkin* and Jon Almack*;

University of Montana Wolf Ecology Project: Robert Ream, Dan Pletscher, and Diane Boyd*;

Individuals with conservation organizations: Hank Fischer* (Defenders of Wildlife), Pat Tucker (National Wildlife Federation), Bobbie Holaday* (Preserve Arizona's Wolves), Elizabeth Sizemore* (Mexican Wolf Coalition of Texas), Carol Martindale (Mexican Wolf Coalition of New Mexico), Nicholas Lapham and Molly Clayton (the Wolf Fund), Nicole Whittington-Evans* (the Alaska Wildlife Alliance), Michael Robinson* (Sinapu);

Jack Gladstone* (Blackfeet Indian singer/songwriter/brother to the wolf), Jay Vest (expert on Native stories on wolves), Margaret Murie, Louise Murie-MacLoed (widow of Adolph Murie), Jenny Ryon* and Shelley Alexander* (wolf biologists in Nova Scotia), Paul Paquet* (wolf biologist in Canada), Rolf Peterson* (Director of the Isle Royale wolf study), Susan Bragdon,* Kent Newton (Rio Grande Zoo in Albuquerque), Curt Mullis (Director, New Mexico Animal Damage Control), H. Alan Foster (Director, Colorado Animal Damage Control), Congressman Wayne Owens (Utah), and Mary Flaming* (Yellowstone Association); Kathy Schaff (Alaska Tourism Marketing Council).

The names marked with an asterisk indicate people who reviewed portions of the text for accuracy. Their comments and suggestions saved me from many errors and greatly improved the book. I am very grateful to them for their help. I particularly wish to thank Diane Boyd, Norm Bishop, and Steve Fritts for the substantial amount of time they spent helping me. My editors, Elizabeth Knight and Helene Anderson, deserve a lot of credit for improving the text. Any errors are mine, of course.

Because this book is intended for a general readership rather than a scholarly audience, I limited my listing of references. The books named in the section "References and Suggested Readings on Wolves" represent my major sources. Within the text I mention the names of other writers and biologists whose work was helpful. Information on wolf control in the national parks came from National Park Service reports available for public study in the archives at Denali, Yellowstone, and Glacier national parks, and at the National Park Service Regional Office at Denver. The reports by William Brown (Denali), John Weaver (Yellowstone), and Francis Singer (Glacier) were especially helpful in documenting that period of persecution.

I would also like to thank the staff at the following libraries: University of Alaska, University of California Berkeley, University of California Riverside, University of Nevada Las Vegas, University of New Mexico, University of Wyoming, Colorado State University, the Montana Historical Society, the Wyoming State Archives, the South Dakota State Historical Society, the Alaska Resources Library and the Palm Desert Library. Thanks also to Lorie Bacon, Angela Tripp, Raquel Rivera-Bertrand, Elizabeth Dirks, Alan McIntyre, and Elaine Boni.

All of my photos were taken with Minolta cameras and lenses. The following Minolta Corporation employees arranged loans of equipment that greatly helped in my photography: Doug Dodge, Bill Suarez, Phil Bradon, Karen Calissi, and Carolle Sluszniak.

Lastly, a special thanks to Jay Deist and Lew Lowery for their expert help in wolf photography.

About the Author

(Photo by Clark Mishler.)

Rick McIntyre cites Thoreau's *Walden* as a primary reason he is thoroughly devoted to the study of wildlife and nature. He's made his own additions to the world's nature library by authoring *Denali National Park: An Island in Time* (Albion Publishing Group, 1986), and *Grizzly Cub: Five Years in the Life of a Bear* (Alaska Northwest Books, 1990).

He has worked as a park ranger for a total of eighteen years in such areas as Denali National Park, Glacier National Park, and Death Valley National Monument. During his off-duty hours in Denali and Glacier, McIntyre has spent thousands of hours watching wild wolves. Nature photography is another of McIntyre's talents. His photographs have appeared in over 150 books and in numerous magazines. Like Thoreau, McIntyre has no permanent home, but goes wherever his interest in wildlife and nature takes him.

A portion of the author's royalties from the sale of this book will be donated to the wolf organizations mentioned on page 119.